Samuel French Acting Edition

Paddywack

A Drama in Two Acts

by Daniel Magee

SAMUELFRENCH.COM   SAMUELFRENCH.CO.UK

Copyright © 1996 by Daniel Magee
All Rights Reserved

PADDYWACK is fully protected under the copyright laws of the United States of America, the British Commonwealth, including Canada, and all other countries of the Copyright Union. All rights, including professional and amateur stage productions, recitation, lecturing, public reading, motion picture, radio broadcasting, television and the rights of translation into foreign languages are strictly reserved.

ISBN 978-0-573-69578-0

www.SamuelFrench.com
www.SamuelFrench.co.uk

FOR PRODUCTION ENQUIRIES

UNITED STATES AND CANADA
Info@SamuelFrench.com
1-866-598-8449

UNITED KINGDOM AND EUROPE
Plays@SamuelFrench.co.uk
020-7255-4302

Each title is subject to availability from Samuel French, depending upon country of performance. Please be aware that *PADDYWACK* may not be licensed by Samuel French in your territory. Professional and amateur producers should contact the nearest Samuel French office or licensing partner to verify availability.

CAUTION: Professional and amateur producers are hereby warned that *PADDYWACK* is subject to a licensing fee. Publication of this play(s) does not imply availability for performance. Both amateurs and professionals considering a production are strongly advised to apply to Samuel French before starting rehearsals, advertising, or booking a theatre. A licensing fee must be paid whether the title(s) is presented for charity or gain and whether or not admission is charged. Professional/Stock licensing fees are quoted upon application to Samuel French.

No one shall make any changes in this title(s) for the purpose of production. No part of this book may be reproduced, stored in a retrieval system, or transmitted in any form, by any means, now known or yet to be invented, including mechanical, electronic, photocopying, recording, videotaping, or otherwise, without the prior written permission of the publisher. No one shall upload this title(s), or part of this title(s), to any social media websites.

For all enquiries regarding motion picture, television, and other media rights, please contact Samuel French.

MUSIC USE NOTE

Licensees are solely responsible for obtaining formal written permission from copyright owners to use copyrighted music in the performance of this play and are strongly cautioned to do so. If no such permission is obtained by the licensee, then the licensee must use only original music that the licensee owns and controls. Licensees are solely responsible and liable for all music clearances and shall indemnify the copyright owners of the play(s) and their licensing agent, Samuel French, against any costs, expenses, losses and liabilities arising from the use of music by licensees. Please contact the appropriate music licensing authority in your territory for the rights to any incidental music.

IMPORTANT BILLING AND CREDIT REQUIREMENTS

If you have obtained performance rights to this title, please refer to your licensing agreement for important billing and credit requirements.

PADDYWACK

A play by DANIEL MAGEE

*Paddywack was originally presented as a co-production
between William Butler-Sloss, Kate Percival
and the Soho Theatre Company at the Cockpit Theatre, London.
The first performance of the play was on March 1st 1994.*

Richard Trahair	*Colin*
Brian Croucher	*Brian*
Michael O'Hagan	*Michael*
Doreen Andrew	*Mrs. Somers*
James Neabitt	*Damien*
Holly Aird	*Annette*
Michael Latimer	*Director*
Mark Viner	*Design*
Alex Watherston	*Costumes*
Chris Davey	*Lighting*
Colin Brown	*Sound*

*The author would like to acknowledge the help and advice
given to him by Michael Latimer
during the early part of writing this play.*

LONG WHARF THEATRE

September 27 – October 30, 1994

The Newton Schenck Stage
PRESENTS

PADDYWACK

by
DANIEL MAGEE

Directed by JOHN TILLINGER
Set Design by JAMES YOUMANS
Costume Design by CANDICE DONNELLY
Lighting Design by KEN BILLINGTON
Production Stage Manager: ARTHUR GAFFIN
Artistic Director: ARVIN BROWN
Executive Director: M. EDGAR ROSENBLUM

Colin	ALESSANDRO NIVOLA
Brian	DENIS O'HARE
Michael	MICHAEL O'HAGAN
Mrs. Somers	PATRICIA KILGARRIFF
Damien	JAMES NESBITT
Annette	SARAH LONG

Casting: Deborah Brown and Susan Shopmaker
Dialect Consultant: Barbara Somerville
Fight Coordinator: Michael Giansanti
Scenic Artist: Keith Hyatte

Paddywack *is produced in association with Flamin' Eejits Ltd.*
Paddywack *was originally produced by William Butler-Sloss, Kate Percival and the Soho Theatre Company at the Cockpit Theatre, London.*

CHARACTERS

COLIN: English, 20s

BRIAN: English, 30s

MICHAEL: Irish, 50s

MRS. SOMERS: English, 60s

DAMIEN: Irish, 20s

ANNETTE: English, 20s

SETTING

London, the present.

The set can be open plan – defined by areas of light.

Scene changes can be effected by the actors in view of the audience

ACT I

Scene One

(The play opens in a lodging house [digs] with four beds in it. There is a locker by each bed. A man is lying on one of the beds reading a book. By another bed a man is sitting writing. On one of the beds there is a suitcase and some wrapped packages.)

COLIN: *(Reading. He is about twenty one and English)* What's the time, Brian?

BRIAN: *(Also an Englishman, a Cockney)* Quarter past.

COLIN: Quarter past what?

BRIAN: *(Looks at COLIN)* Eight ... And it's Tuesday ... And it's the 17th October, and it's raining, OK?

COLIN: You seen him yet?

BRIAN: *(Looks towards the suitcases and packages)* No ... He dropped them in earlier.

COLIN: *(Looks up at BRIAN from behind his book)* Oh ... I wonder what he's like ...

BRIAN: 'aven't a clue, mate ... But I can tell you one thing,

COLIN: *(Watching him)* Yeah?

BRIAN: Yeah, 'ee's a foreign gentleman

(He looks at COLIN with a "knowing" smile.)

COLIN: *(Not sure what to make of BRIAN's attitude)* Yeah ... So?

BRIAN: Do you not want to know what "brand"?

COLIN: *(A bit annoyed and unsure)* What are you looking at me like that for ... It makes no difference to me ...

(After looking at BRIAN for a while, who does not answer, he lifts the book to his face again.)

BRIAN: *(Smiling)* Tell you what, Colin ... I'll give you a clue.

COLIN: *(From behind his book)* Don't bother.

BRIAN: *(Ignoring him)* Let's see now ... Yes, I've got it ... I'll give you the first letter of his nationality, OK?

COLIN: *(Still from behind his book)* If you haven't met him how would you know?

BRIAN: Missus Somers told me ... Now, do you want the clue or do you want to try for maximum points by guessing straight out?

COLIN: Oh, piss off, Brian.

BRIAN: So, you do want the clue ... You'll lose bonus points ... *(He pretends to read from a card in his hand, game-show wise)* The subject's nationality begins with the letter ... *(Pauses)* "P" ... *(Pauses)* I am also allowed to tell you that there are a lot of them around ... A hell of a lot ... *(There is dead silence as BRIAN regards COLIN, who remains still)* Come on, mate ... I thought that that would be dead easy for a brainy bloke like you ... How many foreign type folk is there who's nationality begins with a "P"? Tell you what, to make it easier ... but at the expense of more bonus points, I'm afraid ... I'll rule out Puerto Ricans and Peruvians ... Come on, have a stab at it ...

COLIN: *(Still from behind his book)* Very amusing ... Anyway, I don't believe you ...

BRIAN: What don't you believe?

COLIN: *(Lowers his book)* If what you're making such a meal of suggesting were true I somehow don't think you'd find it so amusing.

BRIAN: OK ... If you don't want to believe me you don't have to. I just thought I'd warn you ...

(He lifts his letter again and makes as though he is very engrossed.)

(After a short time, COLIN lowers his book and looks at BRIAN, who is "preoccupied" with his letter. He then looks towards the new-comer's bed. He returns his attention to his book. After a time he puts the book down. He looks irritated.)

COLIN: You are kidding, aren't you, Brian?

BRIAN: *(Mock puzzlement)* Kidding? ... About what?

COLIN: *(Irritably)* Knock it off, will you ... About this new guy being a Pakistani ... ?

BRIAN: *(Mock astonishment)* A what ... Who said anything about him being a Paki?

COLIN: *(Lifts his book again)* Oh, sod off ...

BRIAN: The clue was that his nationality began with a "P" ... and so it does ... The gentleman's a Paddy.

COLIN: Irish?

BRIAN: A Paddy. Like Shakespeare said, a Paddy by any other name is still a Paddy.

COLIN: I might have known you'd be twisting things.

BRIAN: Yeah, well ... adds to the enjoyment, don't it

Colin. *(Turns and stares straight at COLIN)* I mean ... you wouldn't be enjoying that great sense of relief you are right now if it hadn't been for the bit of a tease, now would you?

COLIN: *(Looks serious)* I don't think I quite follow you ...

BRIAN: Oh, don't you?

COLIN: No ... exactly what are you suggesting, Brian?

BRIAN: Come off it, will you ... I saw you ... As soon as I said "P" and you thought "Paki" ... you gave out vibes you could bend a spoon with.

COLIN: That's ...

BRIAN: *(Cuts in)* ... a fact.

COLIN: Rubbish. In the first place I didn't believe you.

BRIAN: Oh, why not?

COLIN: Well, nice as she is I somehow can't see Mrs. Somers accepting coloured people ... can you ... ?

BRIAN: I don't see why not ... she accepts Paddys.

COLIN: Oh indeed ... Well you seem to get on alright with Michael.

(He nods towards the fourth bed.)

BRIAN: *(Follows his gaze)* Yeah ... but with two of them they might start to breed.

COLIN: Boy ... this really does seem to have you upset.

BRIAN: Don't it never bug you, then?

COLIN: No, ... why should it?

BRIAN: Shit.

COLIN: Why is that "shit"?

BRIAN: I'll tell you why ... 'cause for a moment there ... when you did think I meant a Paki ... your little "liberal" heart skipped a beat.

COLIN: That's bloody nonsense ... Mrs. Somers could fill the house with "Pakis", as you put it ... and I wouldn't give a damn ... Not that there's much danger of that.

BRIAN: *(Smiles broadly)* Exactly ...

COLIN: *(Attempts a response)* Whaa ...

BRIAN: Which is why you're here.

COLIN: *(Highly insulted)* That's bloody outrageous ...

BRIAN: *(Continues as though not interrupted)* It's why we're all here ... Including Michael.

COLIN: Who are you to say why any of us are here ... You most certainly can't speak for me ... As far as Michael goes ...

BRIAN: *(Cuts in)* The pub.

COLIN: *(Somewhat confused by this remark)* What?

BRIAN: The pub ... That's as far as Michael goes.

COLIN: You've an answer for everything, haven't you.

BRIAN: That would never do, would it ... An 'umble tradesman having an answer to "anything" ... not when we've got educated chaps like you around to know everything for us.

COLIN: There's more to it than "knowing" ... There's "caring".

BRIAN: Blimey, look who's talking ... A minute ago you were going on about just how much you didn't care ... As far as you were concerned that ol' bag, Somers could fill the house with bleeding Zulus and you wouldn't care ... Not caring seems to be the main function of you so-called liberal bastards.

COLIN: You would have me a "racist" bastard I suppose.

BRIAN: I wouldn't have you if you paid me, ol' son ... Besides, I don't hate Pakis, or Paddys ... I just don't see the need for 'em ... Not now-a-days what with robots and the like ...

COLIN: *(Incensed)* You arrogant, fucking ...

(We hear the sound of someone approaching the room.)

BRIAN: *(Holding a finger up to his lips)* Now, now, Colin ... we don't want to upset the nice new paddy man ... *(Jerks his thumb towards the door)* ... do we?

COLIN: *(Lies back in bed and lowers his voice)* I hope he's six foot four and bright green all over.

(The door opens and a middle-aged man enters. COLIN and BRIAN look at him.)

BRIAN: Michael, ... how are you?

MICHAEL: *(Senses atmosphere)* How am I?

BRIAN: Well, how would you like to be six foot four and bright green all over?

MICHAEL: *(Looks at BRIAN and then at COLIN and back to BRIAN again)* That's the stupidest fucking question I've heard all night, and I've heard some crackers ... I've just left Molloy in the pub because he was driving me spare talking shite about boxing ... I hope you're not trying to drive me bloody back.

BRIAN: Wouldn't dream of it mate.

MICHAEL: *(Unlacing his shoes while sitting on the edge of the bed)* Do you know what he was telling me ... He held that if it hadn't been for the bell, Henry Cooper would have beaten Cassius Clay ... He even ...

COLIN: *(Interrupts from behind his book)* Mohammed Ali.

MICHAEL: *(Looks around at him somewhat quizzically)* What? ... Oh aye ...

BRIAN: How do you know he wouldn't have?

MICHAEL: What? ... Beat Clay? ... No bloody way ...

COLIN: *(Louder)* Ali.

BRIAN: *(Turns irritably on COLIN)* Ali-fucking-pally.

COLIN: *(Lowers his book and addresses BRIAN)* Listen ... the man chose to be called Ali ... is it asking too much for people to respect his basic right ...

MICHAEL: I don't give a damn what he's called, when he came back after that knockdown he nearly took Cooper apart at the seams.

COLIN: You just don't give a damn, do you?

MICHAEL: What's up with you tonight ... As far as I'm concerned if Cassius Clay was good enough to Christen him by it's good enough for me to call him by.

COLIN: That is the whole bloody point ... The man chose to no longer be a bloody Christian ... That's what his change of name signified ... It meant something. If he were a film star and changed his name to Fifi-la-bloody-Fluff everybody would be breaking their necks to get it right.

MICHAEL: *(Taken aback by COLIN's passion)* Jesus Christ the night ... "Fifi-La-Fluff" ... You're beginning to sound like Molloy. I went into the pub tonight in the fond hope and naive expectation of a few nice pints ... judicially punctuated with a couple of shots ... and I'm driven ... no ... "washed" out of the place on a tidal wave of bullshite from Molloy ... only to find that now it's a bloody epidemic. *(He notices the case and packages)* What's all this then?

BRIAN: Like I was telling you we're expecting someone.

MICHAEL: Oh aye ... A new lodger?
BRIAN: Yeah.
MICHAEL: Well, let's hope he doesn't talk bloody nonsense.
BRIAN: Oh, I reckon you'll get along all right with him ... Won't he Colin?

(COLIN ignores BRIAN.)

MICHAEL: Oh aye?
BRIAN: Michael ... he's a Paki.
MICHAEL: *(Gets up slowly and goes over and looks at the gear on the bed)* Is he having me on, Colin?
COLIN: *(After looking at the smiling BRIAN)* Why ... would it make any difference?
MICHAEL: Well I'd say it would.
BRIAN: Not to Colin, here.
COLIN: *(To MICHAEL)* And you were the one going on about how great Mohammed Ali was.
BRIAN: He's got a point there, Michael ... You was going on.
MICHAEL: Oh aye ... And have you ever heard me going on about how great Secretariat was ... It doesn't mean I want him in the bed next to me.
COLIN: *(Turns to BRIAN)* I think this has gone on long enough.
BRIAN: Oh shut up, Colin ... Well, what do you reckon we should do about it, Michael?
MICHAEL: Do? ... I know what I'm going to do ... What's come over the old cow anyway ... Is she that short of shillings. I could have got her any amount of clean, decent lads to take the shagging bed.

COLIN: *(Angered)* And what makes you assume that black people aren't clean ... or decent?

MICHAEL: Have you ever been captured on the Undergroud beside any of 'em? You'd swear that they were all armpit ... *(He goes towards the door)* I'm gonna have a word with that stupid aul bitch.

COLIN: *(Alarmed, jumps up)* Now, hold on, Michael.

(He steps in front of MICHAEL.)

MICHAEL: *(Pushes COLIN aside)* Out of my way ...

(Exits)

COLIN: *(Walking about, agitated)* Christ, Brian ... Now look what you've done ...

BRIAN: *(Laughing)* I've done? ... It was you who defended our Paki room-mate.

COLIN: A joke's a joke ... but now he'll go down roaring and shouting at Mrs. Somers and kick up God knows what trouble before he finds out the truth.

BRIAN: *(Laughing)* Yeah.

COLIN: That's what you want, isn't it ... God, I might have known ... If he goes too far she might chuck him out, right?

BRIAN: So, what's it to you ... He's only another racist bastard.

COLIN: He's a stupid bloody fool listening to you.

BRIAN: I didn't say he was an intelligent racist bastard.

Scene Two

(Mrs. Somers' kitchen. MRS. SOMERS is sitting reading the paper and having a cup of tea. She is elderly but fit looking.)
(MICHAEL, off-stage, yells, "Mrs. Somers ... Mrs. Somers!". She looks up when MICHAEL enters. He looks earnest.)

MRS. SOMERS: Michael ... what are you after?

MICHAEL: It's about this new lodger, Mrs. Somers ...

MRS. SOMERS: Oh, were the lads telling you?

MICHAEL: I just found out this minute ... I couldn't believe me ears ...

MRS. SOMERS: *(Somewhat puzzled)* You couldn't? ... About what?

MICHAEL: I'm sure you know damned well what about ...

MRS. SOMERS: *(Sharply)* You can keep that language for your work-mates, if you please, and explain yourself.

MICHAEL: Me explain ... It's you who should be doing the explaining ... It's me you've landed him up beside.

MRS. SOMERS: What, or who are you blethering on about, man?

MICHAEL: Gunga-Bloody-Din, that's who ...

(At this point a young man enters behind MICHAEL, who, in his rage, does not notice him.)

MRS. SOMERS: And who, when he's home, might that be?

MICHAEL: You might as well say "at home" ...

(Splutters) You've given him the bed next to mine as his bloody home ... I suppose there's another truck-load of them arriving next week ...

DAMIEN: *(Who has been standing feeling awkward in the meantime)* I'll drop back later ...

(Goes to exit.)

MRS. SOMERS: *(Calling to stop him leaving)* No, no lad ... Just hang on a minute, till I can make head or tail of what Michael here is raving on about ... *(Turns her attention on MICHAEL)* Now, start again, Michael ...

MICHAEL: *(Who has been staring at DAMIEN since he noticed him)* Who's he?

MRS. SOMERS: Well if you stop ranting and raving I'll introduce you ... This is Damien ... your room-mate ...

MICHAEL: *(Looking DAMIEN up and down)* New room-mate?

MRS. SOMERS: Yes.

MICHAEL: *(Still staring at DAMIEN)* What about the Paki?

MRS. SOMERS: What Paki?

MICHAEL: The one Brian was telling me about.

MRS. SOMERS: Brian? ... So that's what all this is about ... Are you ever going to wise up to him?

MICHAEL: The bastard ... *(He then addresses DAMIEN as he extends his hand to him)* ... I'm sorry lad ... what's your name? ... Oh aye, it's Damien, isn't it ... I'm sorry ... you're welcome ... *(He then turns to MRS. SOMERS)* I'm sorry Missus Somers, but I got an awful shock ... *(He exits abruptly)* *(From off-stage we can hear MICHAEL shouting up the stairs ahead of himself as he goes.)* You thin faced English bastard ... just wait 'til I get me hands on you.

MRS. SOMERS: Well lad, you've come in at the deep end ... Brian, one of the lads you'll be sharing with must have been pulling his leg about you being a Paki ...

DAMIEN: *(After having listened to this and, smiling bewilderedly, returns his attention to MRS. SOMERS)* A Paki?

MRS. SOMERS: Yes ... A Pakistani ... But then I don't expect you'd have seen a lot of then where you come from ...

DAMIEN: No, not a lot ... I'm sorry if I busted in ... I was just after the key to the room.

MRS. SOMERS: No, not at all ... As a matter of fact it's just as well you did ... For Michael's sake ... he tends to fly off the handle ... Him and Brian are the best of mates really. You'll see, when you get up there the pair of them will be having a right old laugh ... *(In the meantime she has gone to a shelf and taken down a key)* Here, I had it cut down the market this morning.

DAMIEN: Oh, thanks ... How much do I owe you?

MRS. SOMERS: Don't worry, dear ... you're paying for it in your rent.

DAMIEN: *(About to leave)* Great, thanks ... I'll just be ...

MRS. SOMERS: Here, don't rush off ... Anyroad, you want to give that pair upstairs a bit of time to settle down.

DAMIEN: Thanks ... missus ... ah ...

MRS. SOMERS: "Somers" ...You'll soon get used to it ... And you're Damien ... That's a lovely name ... How come you Irish get all the nice names and we're left wi' Freds and Bills.

DAMIEN: We've plenty of Freds and Bills too ...

Besides, having a nice name isn't always an advantage ... You can get a lot of slagging ... ah, joked about ... I've a mate from Dublin who's called 'Maolise ... and the stick he has to take about it sometimes nearly drives him up the wall.

MRS. SOMERS: 'Maolise ... That sounds nearly too nice for a fella.

DAMIEN: Aye, that's what he thinks ... Mind you he is a nice fella.

MRS. SOMERS: I'm sure he is ... With a name like that he couldn't help it, now could he ... I think things like that can affect you ... Know what I mean ... like being born by the sea. Have you ever noticed that folk born by the sea always seem to be looking far away in the distance ... You take Cockneys, now ... they look at you like you were a fly on the end of their noses ... Shifty looking buggers. Here, I've made you some sandwiches, sit down. I'll just fetch them.

DAMIEN: Oh aye ... You really shouldn't have bothered.

MRS. SOMERS: I've seen enough of you lads over the years to know that you's haven't the wit to feed yourselves when you're away from home ...

DAMIEN: Thanks ...

MRS. SOMERS: You just go on and eat them, lad ... I like to watch a man eat ... Sometimes I think it's all they're good for ... and they think they're ever so sharp.

DAMIEN: Pardon ...

(Not sure as to what she's referring.)

MRS. SOMERS: Cockneys ... If you came from any further away than Barnet they think you come up the river in a bubble.

DAMIEN: It's the same in Belfast.

MRS. SOMERS: Aye lad, but I'm not from country ... I come from Oldham.

DAMIEN: Oldham ... that's where they make batteries, isn't it?

MRS. SOMERS: Aye ... but battery's gone flat ... I suppose that's why you're here yourself ... work?

DAMIEN: Aye ... I needed to get away ... earn some money.

MRS. SOMERS: Anything lined up?

DAMIEN: No, but a friend of mine told me ... well, wrote me, that there might be a chance where he is.

MRS. SOMERS: Oh aye ... and what does your friend do?

DAMIEN: He's a dispatch clerk.

MRS. SOMERS: A dispatch clerk?

DAMIEN: It's not as grand as it sounds ... He loads vans mainly. He says there's a chance they'll be taking people on. He thinks it's a good idea to be on the spot.

MRS. SOMERS: That's the ticket, lad.

DAMIEN: You needn't worry about the rent ... I've enough for a while.

MRS. SOMERS: Don't fret, lad ... as long as you pay your rent your business is your own ... Michael, him you met, he'll be able to help you, being Irish and that ... show you the ropes ... They're all nice lads here ... No messers.

DAMIEN: Great.

MRS. SOMERS: 'Ee's been with me nearly ten year ... Never goes home.

DAMIEN: No?

MRS. SOMERS: Can't understand that ... You'd think

he'd be glad to get away from here once in a while.

DAMIEN: He must like it ... Do you get back home much yourself?

MRS. SOMERS: Me? ... Good Lord, no ... Last time I saw Oldham was when I buried my Jack there ... And I didn't really see Oldham then ... just a big broken, cold lump of it they threw down on top of Jack ... That and this long string of misery of an undertaker ... I remember thinking at the time ... standing there in the graveyard as men were throwing black sods in on top of Jack ... how "unfair" it was ...

DAMIEN: Unfair?

MRS. SOMERS: Jack was a great dancer ... he loved dancing ... and here was this misery guts ... white as lard and twice as mean ... and him burying Jack ... Jack who looked better in his coffin than this creature did out of it. *(Pause)* No, I never went to Oldham again ... But that's different, if you know what I mean ... Well, I'm at home, aren't I?

DAMIEN: Yes ... I suppose you are.

(There is a knock on the door and COLIN puts his head around it.)

COLIN: Mrs. Somers ... is it alright if I borrow the electric kettle?

MRS. SOMERS: Are you going to sit up all night again? And I thought you were supposed to bring one back with you the last time you went home?

COLIN: Yes ... I'm sorry, I forgot it in the rush.

MRS. SOMERS: Rush, huh ... Well, come in lad ... This is Damien, he's your new room-mate ... And I hope you lot haven't done anything fancy wi' 'is bed ... Damien, this is

Colin ... 'ee's brainy one amongst us.
DAMIEN: Hello ...

(Reaches out his hand.)
(MRS. SOMERS goes off to search out the kettle. When she is not looking, COLIN mimics to DAMIEN that she talks a lot.)

COLIN: Have you just arrived?
DAMIEN: Yes, ... this morning.
COLIN: Over for work?
DAMIEN: Hopefully.

(MRS. SOMERS returns with the kettle.)

MRS. SOMERS: *(Handing COLIN the kettle)* Here you are, lad ... and mind you don't burn out the element.
COLIN: Thanks Mrs. Somers ... No, I won't ...
DAMIEN: *(Getting up from his chair)* Here, I'll go up with you, Colin ... Thanks for the sandwiches, Missus Somers.
MRS. SOMERS: Don't mention it ... I enjoyed our little chat ... See you at breakfast ... though I don't expect we'll be seeing you, Colin.
COLIN: Hardly ... Well, goodnight.
DAMIEN: Goodnight.

(He and COLIN exit.)

MRS. SOMERS: Goodnight.

(She clears up and exits.)

PADDYWACK

Scene Three

(The radio is on. Lights come up again in the dining room. It is morning and the table is set for breakfast. MICHAEL and BRIAN are sitting having finished breakfast.)

MICHAEL: Nice.

BRIAN: *(Reading a paper)* What?

MICHAEL: The scrambled eggs ... they were nice.

BRIAN: Yeah.

MICHAEL: Well, what do you think of him?

BRIAN: Who ... Damien ... Can't say as I thought anything. Didn't exactly overwhelm us with his Irish wit, did 'e?

MICHAEL: I suppose he was knackered ... You know, the traveling and getting back late, and all.

BRIAN: Yeah, he was late ... I expect you're glad to see him.

MICHAEL: Who would I be glad to see him ... I was glad to see that he wasn't a Pakistani.

BRIAN: You know what I mean ... Him being Irish and that ... A little bit of the old Country ... He'll be able to bring you up to date with what's happening back home.

MICHAEL: "Bring me up to date"? ... Are you kidding ... He's not from where I'd call "home", he's from across the country somewhere.

BRIAN: Oh, I see. As far as I'm concerned one Irish bloke is much the same as another.

MICHAEL: Both thick, eh?

BRIAN: Now, now, Michael ... I didn't say that.

MICHAEL: Aye, I noticed that ... That you didn't "say" it.

BRIAN: There you are then. *(Calls off)* That tea coming, Mrs. Somers?

MICHAEL: Where am I then?

BRIAN: Well I didn't say something and you noticed right off. Now that ain't thick, is it ... that's bleeding perceptive, if you ask me.

MICHAEL: Is it, indeed?

BRIAN: Yeah ... Like a whole new concept in communication ... Not only are you conscious of what I've just "said", you're conscious ... through a complex process of elimination ... of what I've "not" said as well.

MICHAEL: Aye, that's a trick I picked up over here ... When you're dealing with people who're devious enough to have invented the British Civil Service ... and still refer to it as "civil" ... you learn to read between the lines.

BRIAN: Yeah, well ... we needed it, didn't we ... I mean, we had a Civilization to run, hadn't we?

MICHAEL: "A civilization? From what I remember of the atlas when I was at school you'd half the bloody civilizations in the World to run ... And run them you certainly did ... right into the bloody ground.

BRIAN: Awh, come on now, Michael ... Where would half them poor wogs be if it hadn't been for us.

MICHAEL: Just like yourself, mate ... I don't give a shit ... As far as I'm concerned they're welcome to go back up their bloody trees.

BRIAN: Typical Irish, no sense of responsibility ...

MICHAEL: Responsibility? I remember, as a kid, bringing me pennies into school for the bastards ... We called them "Black Babies" ... I hadn't an arse in me own trousers at the time ... It was supposed to go to building them schools and hospitals ... Little did I know that the bastards were saving it up for the fare over here.

BRIAN: And maybe if you'd been a bit more generous, they'd have had enough money to end up in Ireland instead of over here.

MICHAEL: *(Acknowledges the dig)* Aye ... And if I'd saved it for myself, I'd have had enough money to go to a decent bloody Country ... Like America.

(MRS. SOMERS enters from the kitchen with more tea.)

MRS. SOMERS: America, Michael? Two year ago you were talking about going to Blackpool ... And you've not gone yet. Is it not time you were going to Potter's Bar?

MICHAEL: There's no hurry this morning, they'll still be loading at ten o'clock.

BRIAN: *(Laughing)* Here, Michael ... is it true that you went out there for a job because you thought it was a pub?

MICHAEL: Pub ... I'll pub you ...

MRS. SOMERS: What's got into you two this morning ... *(Nods towards the kitchen)* ... From in there the pair of you sounded like bears wi' sore heads.

MICHAEL: It's that eejit there ... being bloody smart.

BRIAN: Are you calling me an idiot?

MICHAEL: Jasus, you're getting square and good at the old communication yourself, Brian.

MRS. SOMERS: Oh don't start again ... It's like 'aving bloody babies ... Was there any move out of that fella, Colin, when you were coming down?

BRIAN: The professor? The last move I saw outta him was turning pages as I fell asleep.

MRS. SOMERS: I expected as much ... When he takes kettle up he's set for a session wi' books ... Somm'at wouldn't 'ave done you pair any harm when you were 'is age.

MICHAEL: The Wide World, Missus Somers, is book enough for any man ... if he cares to peruse.

MRS. SOMERS: 'appen it is, Michael ... When you get past title page let me know.

MICHAEL: *(Reacting to BRIAN laughing at this)* I don't know what you're laughing at ... If you strayed beyond the sound of Bow bloody Bells you'd think you were on another bloody planet.

BRIAN: At least I can make it as far as Spain for me bleeding 'olidays.

MICHAEL: Oh Spain ... Which part ... The Costa-del-Fish-And-Chips. You could hardly call that "foreign".

BRIAN: Who wants bleeding "foreign" ... That's why I go ... To get away from bleeding foreigners.

MRS. SOMERS: You're some pair.

BRIAN: Pair? With 'im? Do me a favour ...

MICHAEL: Mrs. Somers, please. Sharing a room is one thing, but if ...

MRS. SOMERS: *(Cuts him off)* Oh never mind ... If you're hanging on a bit, Michael, would you mind telling that new chap, Damien, 'ee can do for 'imself ... there's an egg and bacon laid out in the kitchen. I want to get to the Post Office.

MICHAEL: Bacon? Indeed?

MRS. SOMERS: Aye ... there's not many lads as'll bother scrambling eggs ... 'ee can make a fry.

BRIAN: *(Getting up)* I can drop you, if you're ready to move.

MRS. SOMERS: Oh good ... I'll get me coat ...

(Exits to dining room.)

BRIAN: *(Leaning over towards MICHAEL and talking in lowered voice)* 'ere, your mate seems well in ... Do you think maybe 'ee's going to be the cock lodger?

MICHAEL: I thought you were.

BRIAN: Not even with yours, mate. Not even with yours.

(MRS. SOMERS returns with her hat and coat on.)

MRS. SOMERS: Are you sure it's not out of your way, Brian?

BRIAN: Not a bit of it, darling ... What's the use of 'aving wheels if you can't 'elp out a friend, eh?

MRS. SOMERS: You're a real charmer ... I'd say your mother missed you when you left ...

MICHAEL: Aye ... Isn't it a pity she was such a lousy shot.

MRS. SOMERS: Oh, come on or you'll be late for work.

(They both exit, BRIAN making an "up yours" gesture to MICHAEL as he goes. After they have left MICHAEL reaches over and lifts the paper BRIAN was reading. After a time, DAMIEN enters.)

MICHAEL: *(Turning to look at DAMIEN)* Morning ... She left you some bacon and eggs out in the kitchen ... You can help yourself.

DAMIEN: Morning ... That was decent of her. I think I'll

leave it for a minute. Is there any tea in that pot?

MICHAEL: Rakes. I'll get you a mug.

DAMIEN: *(Sitting down at a set place across from MICHAEL and pouring himself tea)* That's great ... I hope it didn't look too ignorant ... me just jumping into bed like that as soon as I arrived.

MICHAEL: No, not at all ... You went out like a light as soon as your head hit the pillow.

DAMIEN: That must have looked terrible ... A total stranger walking into your room and just flaking out.

MICHAEL: Why should it ... It's digs. Sugar?

DAMIEN: The landlady, Mrs. Somers ... she seems a decent sort of woman ...

MICHAEL: She's alright, I suppose ... But mind she doesn't get a hold of you down here ... She'd talk the hind legs off a donkey.

DAMIEN: Aye ... She was telling me about her husband last night.

MICHAEL: Jack? I'll bet set was telling you what a great dancer he was.

DAMIEN: Does she tell everyone about him?

MICHAEL: She tells everyone what a great dancer he was. But do you know something else he was ... He was a bloody good middle-weight. Fought for British Rail ... *(Disparagingly)* Dancing ... To hear Lily you'd think she was married to you man Rudi bloody-fancy-pants, whereas Jack was more like Rocky Marciano ...

DAMIEN: Maybe she liked the Rudi Nureyev side of him better.

MICHAEL: Are you kidding ... I don't care what anybody says ... it was the "man" in him that she went for ...

not some ponce all done up in tights with a jock-strap lashed on to make it look like he'd got balls.

DAMIEN: Boxers wear jock-straps too.

MICHAEL: Aye, to "protect" them ... not to stop them buggering each other ... Have you ever seen them on the telly ... It's bloody embarrassing ... And you don't hear the bible-thumpers going on about them ... Show them a pair of tits and it's like a red rag to a bull ... They don't give a damn about poor chaps like me who don't get the chance very often.

DAMIEN: I thought there was no shortage of that here?

MICHAEL: Don't believe all you've heard over beyond ... Sure they invented half of them stories to encourage young lads like yourself to emigrate just to be shot of you.

DAMIEN: *(Getting up)* I wouldn't put it past them ... I think I'll go and stick that fry on ... Are you sure it's alright?

MICHAEL: Aye, go on ahead. Sure hasn't she left it out for you.

DAMIEN: Right ...

(He exits to kitchen.)

MICHAEL: *(Calling to him)* By the way ... Damien, isn't it?

DAMIEN: *(Off)* Aye ...

MICHAEL: Remember when you came in last night, and I was rearing up ... That was about you ...

DAMIEN: *(Off)* "Me"?

MICHAEL: Well, not really "you" ... You see, Brian told me that the new bloke was a Paki ... So, of course I hit the ceiling.

DAMIEN: Why ... because you thought I was a Pakistani?

(He comes back in.)

MICHAEL: Aye ...

DAMIEN: Why ... Do you not like Pakis?

MICHAEL: Who likes Pakis, except Pakis ... Even them other black bastards don't like them ... Sure, for Jasus sake they can't even stand their own unless they've got the right brand of birdshit on their foreheads ... Can you imagine how I felt when Brian told me that one of them was going to be sharing our room ... Christ ...

DAMIEN: I don't think I can.

MICHAEL: Is this your first time over?

DAMIEN: Aye.

MICHAEL: Well you've a lot to learn. It's not like years ago ... There's parts of this town where they've taken over ... Parts of the whole bloody Country, come to that ...

DAMIEN: So?

MICHAEL: "So?" ... Is that all you can say? So? I don't know about you, but when I bought a ticket over here I didn't bargain for frigging Africa ... or India ... and there's days I'm delivering and that's where I think I frigging am.

DAMIEN: Makes no odds to me ... As far as I'm concerned the whole place is strange.

MICHAEL: Strange ... You want ta tell Brian that ... He's a bleeding cockney and he thinks it's strange ...

DAMIEN: I take it he doesn't like blacks either.

MICHAEL: Do you?

DAMIEN: Sure I don't know any ...

MICHAEL: What's that got to do with it?

DAMIEN: *(Lost for words)* Ah ...

MICHAEL: You don't have to know any of them to know whether you like blacks or not ...

DAMIEN: You don't?

MICHAEL: Let's put it this way ... OK so you don't know any of them personally ... but just imagine if your sister brought a big buck nigger home one night ... What would you think about that ... Eh?

DAMIEN: I don't have a sister ...

MICHAEL: OK, OK ... But just imagine.

DAMIEN: Imagine what?

MICHAEL: Aw, come on Damien ... Stop boxing clever ... you know what I mean. Listen.

DAMIEN: *(Tries to escape)* Ooops, that's my bacon burning. *(Dashes out to kitchen)* ... Ah bollox. *(MICHAEL is impatient to finish his point. We hear DAMIEN in the kitchen cursing and dumping breakfast. DAMIEN returns)* So much for breakfast.

MICHAEL: Aye, right ... Now what was I saying ...

DAMIEN: About my non-existent sister?

MICHAEL: Aye, very amusing Damien ... but what if you had, eh? ... and she landed home with a wog?

DAMIEN: What am I supposed to do now? ... "Imagine" all this happening?

MICHAEL: You said you didn't know any blacks ... Well just think on that and tell me what you'd think of the bastard ...

DAMIEN: OK, Mick isn't it?

MICHAEL: *(Snaps)* Michael, if you don't mind ...

DAMIEN: Michael ... OK ... Let's give this a whirl ... Now ... This sister of mine ... I take it she's mentally retarded?

MICHAEL: *(Thrown)* What?

DAMIEN: Well, bringing a rapist home ... that is what we're talking about ... isn't it?

MICHAEL: Now just a ...

DAMIEN: Either that or she's a whore ... you know ... after his legendary "eighteen inches", eighteen jet black inches. Now you wouldn't want me imagining that about my imaginary wee sister, would you, Michael?

MICHAEL: *(Shaken, angered)* You're fucking sick mate...

DAMIEN: I'm sick ... what are you saying Michael? ... Did I get that wrong or something?

MICHAEL: You think you're so fucking clever don't you?

DAMIEN: Not really ...

MICHAEL: It's easily seen that you've just landed. Just give it six months ... You'll be whistling a different tune then, I'll warrant.

DAMIEN: You reckon?

MICHAEL: Yeah I reckon ...

DAMIEN: So what difference is six months going to make? You said you didn't need to know any of them to know that they're shite ... besides ... I've got my own theory ...

MICHAEL: Oh you have, have you?

DAMIEN: Yeah ... you see Michael, I didn't have to come over here to encounter all that crap ... I've heard it all before at home ... and they didn't even have any over there ... which just goes to prove my theory ...

MICHAEL: So what's this "theory" of yours, smartarse?

DAMIEN: Well it can't be anything to do with jobs ... or housing ... otherwise why would we have it in Ireland ... It's penis envy ... show me a racist and I'll show you a man with a wee dick ...

MICHAEL: Are you taking the fucking piss or what?

DAMIEN: Were you taking the piss about the "Paki" you thought was moving into your room?

MICHAEL: Oh I see ... you're one of these "New Age Paddys" ... all liberal shite and Marxism?

DAMIEN: Marxism ... the only Marx I know is a wee man from the arse end of County Down called Jimmy Marks ... Do you know what his philosophy is? ... He takes people as he finds them ... and he's been all over the world as a seaman ... but then God must have been good to him where he doesn't carry his brains ...

MICHAEL: What are you saying ...

DAMIEN: ... and you want to see him ... he's an ugly wee bastard and he still has to carry a big stick to beat off the women ... so them "big buck niggers" you're on about don't bug him at all. And you won't find him ranting and raving about fucking genocide ... *(Deliberately patronizing)* That big word means ...

MICHAEL: *(Snaps)* If you've finished lecturing ... Look, you're only in this Country five fucking minutes and you're going to start telling me about niggers ...

DAMIEN: I might be only five minutes here but I'm well qualified to talk about "niggers" ... I am a fucking nigger. England made me one.

MICHAEL: Huh, and I thought you were an Irishman.

DAMIEN: Yeah, ... And that fella with "my sister" thought he was her boyfriend ... Especially after she brought him home, and everything ... But we know different, don't we ...

MICHAEL: Listen, son ... if you want to get on in this country you'll have to change your attitude.

DAMIEN: Oh, I see ... Do you mean like if I join the Klu Klux Klan, and keep me nose clean I too could still be in these digs when I'm fifty.

MICHAEL: *(Point taken)* I'll tell you one thing, smart arse ... I'd let no man call me nigger.

DAMIEN: I know ... But sure you'd let no man call you Mick, even.

MICHAEL: What's that supposed to mean? My name is Michael.

DAMIEN: I know. Sure my name's Damien. But I've mates in Dublin and all they ever call me is Damo ... I don't get my knickers in a twist about it. What's wrong with Mick ... it was good enough for Collins.

MICHAEL: Aye ... but he wasn't living over here. Wait 'til you get out and about and they start calling you Paddy ... How do you think you're going to feel about it?

DAMIEN: Like any man who's name it isn't ... Pissed off.

MICHAEL: Aye, well ... I'll no more let them call me Mick than you would ... *(He notices DAMIEN laughing quietly to himself)* What the hell are you smirkin' at?

DAMIEN: Nothing.

(We hear MRS. SOMERS returning.)

MICHAEL: Listen, mate ... I've been in these digs a long time. I'm well got ... Now you're the first other Irish bloke to move in ... I hope you're not going to make a bollox of it ... We get on just fine here ... We don't need trouble.

DAMIEN: Who does?

(MRS. SOMERS enters.)

MRS. SOMERS: Michael ... are you still here ... Ah, good morning Damien ... Did you get breakfast?

DAMIEN: Yes, thanks ... It was very nice of you to leave it out for me.

MRS. SOMERS: Good, good ... Have you been chatting with Michael here ... I expect 'ee's been telling you what an ol' fusspot landlady is.

MICHAEL: *(Rising, unsmiling)* I'd better be going.

MRS. SOMERS: Aye ... and about time too. They must like you a lot out in Potters Bar letting you wander in at this time of the day.

DAMIEN: *(To MICHAEL)* Oh, do you work in a pub?

MRS. SOMERS: No, lad ... it's a warehouse ... *(Turns to MICHAEL)* Michael, you might be able to put in a word for Damien. *(Moves towards the kitchen, taking her coat off)* I'm putting kettle on, I'm fair whacked.

MICHAEL: *(Waits until she's left the room before bending over DAMIEN and talking in a lowered voice)* Do you not have anything lined up yet?

DAMIEN: *(Looks surprised)* Nothing ... No ...

MICHAEL: Well that's all we need here ... a bloody scrounging Paddy.

DAMIEN: Scrounging Paddy?

MICHAEL: *(Still in a lowered voice)* Aye, scrounging ... sitting around on your arse all day drawing the dole. I suppose that's where you were all yesterday ... signing on?

DAMIEN: Yeah, I signed on ... What about it?

MICHAEL: Didn't lose any bloody time, did you ... Well do me a favour, don't broadcast it all over the house.

DAMIEN: I've no intention of broadcasting anything ... Nor have I any intention of making a secret of how I'm fixed either ... And Michael, you can do me a favour too ... Don't go feeling ashamed on my behalf ... I can do that for meself ... if there's cause ... Alright?

MICHAEL: Do you know something ... If there was a chance out where I am I wouldn't bother me bollox even telling you.

DAMIEN: I'm just going to see if I can get by without your help then ... Or your "advice" ... aren't I?

MICHAEL: Yeah ... *(He then shouts into the kitchen)* I'm off, Missus Somers ... I'll see you later.

MRS. SOMERS: *(Entering from kitchen)* Oh, alright then, Michael. Are you eating at the canteen?

MICHAEL: Yeah ...

(Exits)

MRS. SOMERS: Well now, Damien how did you get on wi' Michael?

DAMIEN: Fine ... just fine.

MRS. SOMERS: Aye ... 'ee's a nice lad.

(They exit.)

Scene Four

(ANNETTE's flat. As the lights go up, ANNETTE is talking on the entryphone.)

ANNETTE: Just push it, Colin ... it's been sticking for some reason.

(She returns to where she was sitting.)
(A short time later COLIN enters. He is breezy and cheerful.)

COLIN: *(Rubbing his hands)* It's freezing out there ... *(He notices some papers lying on the table, and looks through them)* Ah, that piece on nuclear dumping ... They're not using it?

(ANNETTE takes the papers out of his hand, and dumps them in the wastepaper basket.)

ANNETTE: Do you want coffee?
COLIN: Wine's fine.

(Reading a letter which was with the papers.)
(Hands him a glass of wine.)

ANNETTE: Here.
COLIN: *(Cheerful, positive)* It says in the letter ...
ANNETTE: I know what it says in the letter ...
COLIN: Listen darling, you have to have a bit of patience ... It takes time to break into journalism. At least the editor was positive ...
ANNETTE: Colin, I'm not *trying* to break into journalism.
COLIN: *(Can't resist a tease)* Oh ... silly old me ... there I was thinking that submitting about ten articles a week sort of hinted that maybe you were ...

ANNETTE: For someone who thinks of himself as radical, you do come out with some startlingly true-blue perceptions.

COLIN: Such as?

ANNETTE: Your perception of journalism for one.

COLIN: *(Amused at her annoyance)* Oh, I see ...

ANNETTE: No. That's the point, Colin. You don't see. This positive little note from the editor which impressed you so much ... this was the "pat" ... you know, as in "pat-on-the-head" ... as in "patronizing" ... That little prick thinks I'm trying to break into journalism too.

COLIN: Whereas?

ANNETTE: I was *trying* to communicate a specific piece of information ... Namely, that the Irish Sea is being turned into nuclear soup ... *That* is what I was attempting to do. *Not* break into bourgeois bloody so-called journalism ...

COLIN: OK, OK, ... I'm sorry I ...

ANNETTE: And that's what I mean about your perception of it ... The megalomaniacal little pricks who control journalism ... seem to think news, people's lives, and what happens to them, is only there to give *them* something to do ... Not the other bloody way about.

COLIN: OK, ... I surrender, I'm sorry.

ANNETTE: I wasted nearly two months digging up hard, facts that point to the fact that if we don't get our collective finger out, we're all going to end up bloody glow-worms ... And what's the reaction? "Have patients" ... *(Exasperated)* God ... Next you'll be telling me that Anne Landesman is a fucking journalist, *just* because she has a job on a newspaper.

COLIN: *(Hands ANNETTE the wine bottle)* Here, hit me over the head with this ...

ANNETTE: *(His gesture works – her anger expelled, she becomes suddenly tender, smiles)* Would it do any good?

COLIN: I could always tell them back at the lodgings that I was brawling ... It might even help my image, improve my credibility.

ANNETTE: If you took it back to the lodgings and used it to beat the crap out of that fascist, it would do a lot *more* for your credibility ... but of course that wouldn't fit in with your philosophy of patience, would it?

COLIN: He already is having the crap knocked out of him ... metaphorically, anyway ... by the new guy.

ANNETTE: Metaphorical doesn't count ... Like you living there doesn't count.

COLIN: *(Laughs)* What the hell is that supposed to mean?

ANNETTE: Your stupid thesis ... and the idea that you're going to get some sort of insight by slumming it.

COLIN: I'm not slumming it, as you put it. In the first place, it isn't a slum, and ...

ANNETTE: And in the second place, compared to what you are used to, it's a pig sty. And like your hero George Orwell, the whole exercise is somewhat invalidated by the fact that you have a return ticket.

COLIN: Oh, come on Annette ... So you've had a setback, but you, yourself are a writer ... a better one than I am ... Are you trying to tell me that Orwell didn't make any contribution?

ANNETTE: He made a contribution alright ... to the "body academia" ...

COLIN: *(Annoyed)* As opposed to the "body journalese" ... Sorry, I didn't mean that.

ANNETTE: Don't apologize. It was a fair comment ... But can't you see that I don't want to be a "good journalist". Journalism is a means to an end ... theoretically anyway. For every probing reporter there are fifty Robin Leach's turning out pap ... "the-world-as-fruit-flavoured-semolina".

COLIN: I can see that you're a bit pissed off.

ANNETTE: *(Relaxes, smiles)* Does it show?

COLIN: A tiny bit, yes ... Listen would you like to meet Damien?

ANNETTE: The metaphorical warrior?

COLIN: Yea, but I've been watching him and listening to him, and I reckon there's more to him than meets the eye. I don't think he's as metaphorical as all that.

ANNETTE: No? ... Just *how* unmetaphorical is he?

COLIN: We-ell ... let's put it this way, I think he's leap-frogged all the processes which frustrate you so much.

ANNETTE: Does that mean he's not writing a thesis?

COLIN: You don't give up, do you? ... No, he's not writing a thesis ... Nor is he writing articles for the bourgeois press.

ANNETTE: Touché, babe ... teeth.

COLIN: I didn't ...

ANNETTE: *(Quickly) Don't,* whatever you do, apologize ... if this Damien character has shaken your theoretical approach a little bit, then maybe he is worth meeting.

COLIN: I think you'll like him ... and ... surprisingly enough, he doesn't seem to think I'm a twit.

ANNETTE: *(Frowns)* And is that what you think I think?

COLIN: What *do* you think?

ANNETTE: You're a twit. *(Laughs)* Sorry, I couldn't

resist that ... no. An innocent maybe. The "Vincent" of Don McClean's ballad "Come away, Oh human child ..." Or is that Yeats?

COLIN: It's Yeats ... and I'm not sure I like the reference ... the person issuing the invite is a fairy.

ANNETTE: Oh my, we *are* maturing ... a little touch of honest-to-goodness bigotry ... There's hope for you yet. *(Stands)* Come on, let's eat ...

COLIN: *(Rising)* When are you going to start cooking?

ANNETTE: When are *you*?

(They exit as lights fade.)

Scene Five

(The bunk room. It is five weeks later.)

COLIN: How are you settling into the job?

DAMIEN: It's alright ... It's just that the shift work is hard to get used to.

COLIN: I'm sure ... I don't think I'd fancy it.

DAMIEN: You'll likely never have to.

COLIN: Never mind, you might get something better ... What do you think of here?

DAMIEN: What, the digs? ... Not bad ...

COLIN: And the guys?

DAMIEN: Brian and Michael? ... Two fucking gobshites ... Still, as long as they leave me alone I'll leave them alone ... It's man's inalienable right to be a gobshite ... I'm sure thousands have fought and died for it.

COLIN: At least you're able to handle them.

DAMIEN: Meaning you can't ... I don't know why you're here, anyway. It's obvious your people have a few bob ... So what are you doing in a kip like this?

COLIN: I've told you ... A postgraduate thesis.

DAMIEN: Yeah, I know it's to do with post-industrial whatever. But why here? ... You spend most of your time in libraries and reading statistics ... you don't have to live in a place like this to do that.

COLIN: I also spend a lot of time interviewing people whose trades have disappeared, or changed ... and do you know what the most common characteristic I come across is ... bitterness. *(Puts on bad working class accent)* "... and what the fuck would you know about it? ..." and "... it's alright for you mate, going back to your posh bleeding house ..."

DAMIEN: So you tell them that you live in post-Victorian tat with two members of the Kilburn KKK and they open their hearts to you ...

COLIN: Not quite Damien, but it has shut a few mouths in the London School of Economics ... besides, my father never thought I'd stick it ...

DAMIEN: If my folks had the few bob yours have, I'd stick it ... as far as it would go.

COLIN: You really dislike it that much?

DAMIEN: What's to like ... I'm not going to be around that long anyway.

COLIN: *(Equivocally)* Oh? At times I quite fancy it ... The lads can be quite funny ...

DAMIEN: So can Benny Hill, but would you fancy living with him?

COLIN: I'm convinced that half of this "racism" is put on just to get my goat ... I'm just starting to ignore it ...

DAMIEN: Are you, indeed? Doesn't mean it'll ignore you ... Here, Colin, what does Brian say about the Irish ... You know, when me or Michael aren't around?

COLIN: Ah, nothing much ...

DAMIEN: Ooh ... that bad?

COLIN: *(Quickly)* No, honestly ... You know Brian ... he doesn't mean anything by it I'm sure ...

DAMIEN: Oh I know Brian alright ... And he means it ... Don't get your knickers in a twist, Colin ... I've more to worry about than shites like him ... But what do you think of Michael?

COLIN: Well he's not as bad as Brian.

DAMIEN: Isn't he? ... You study things like that, don't you ... Sociology and the like ... What's his game?

COLIN: Game?

DAMIEN: Aye, what's he playing at?

COLIN: I don't follow you.

DAMIEN: Jesus, Colin ... I thought that might have been the only logical reason for you staying here ... Studying guys like them.

COLIN: Actually my field is economics.

DAMIEN: So's Michael's ... How to survive cheek-by-jowl with a shower of racist bastards who see you as an outsider taking their jobs ... Not to mention their women ... that most sensitive of Socio/Racial barometers.

COLIN: Not everybody's like that.

DAMIEN: I know ... but why take a chance ... Get in there right away and let your mates know that you too think the black bastards should be sent packing back to the jungle ... Who knows, if you're convincing enough, they might just overlook the fact that you're a Paddy.

COLIN: I think you're going a bit strong there, Damien. ... From what I've seen the Irish actually seem to be well liked.

DAMIEN: Aye ... as long as they toe the line ... Sure wasn't Michael telling me as much when I first landed ... I've been here five weeks now and not a single day has passed, especially at work, when I haven't heard black people being referred to as though they were shit ... Not one solitary day ... And the Irish blokes there, go right along with it ... Even my mate, and he's more Republican than Gerry Adams.

COLIN: Well I can't say I find the same ... Besides, a lot of it is harmless banter.

DAMIEN: That's what's sick about it ... We're not talking about a minority of fascist dick-heads ... We're talking about your run-of-the-mill, ordinary, decent bloke ... there was this aul fella talking to me in the canteen ... He was a nice aul fella from Sligo, he was telling me about him coming over in the Fifties and about how hard it was to get digs ... you know "Irish need not apply" ... And do you know something ... We hadn't taken two steps outside the canteen when he pointed out this guy going past on a fork-lift and informed me that black bastards like him were going to be the ruination of the Country.

COLIN: *(Alarmed at his passion)* OK, OK, Damien ... I'm not the enemy.

DAMIEN: Yeah, but people from your walk of life don't realize just how deeply ingrained racism is ... but why should you? ... It's unlikely that wherever your people live is going to experience a big influx of coloureds, now is it ... That's why Brian is always having a go at you ... He sees you supporting something which you don't have to live with, but which he does.

COLIN: That's hardly fair ... I live in exactly the same conditions as he does.

DAMIEN: Yeah, but for how long?

COLIN: Just a minute, Damien ... I don't support elitist set-ups which keep social problems outside.

DAMIEN: Do you not ... Brian does ... His only objection is that he's not on the inside ... Michael, the aul eejit, on the other hand, thinks he is on the inside ... And he's quite prepared to do his bit and stand shoulder to shoulder with his adopted Countrymen and kick the living shit out of any "alien" who's considered to threaten it ... Did you not hear him at breakfast about yesterday's bombing at the recruiting office – What he would and would not have done to the scum if he could have laid his hands on them ... Do you know what all that amounted to? ... That was Michael drawing up a huge neon sign saying ... "I didn't do it" ... as if anyone thought he had.

COLIN: Well, you understand that under the circumstances.

DAMIEN: What circumstances ... Brian sitting there ... And if you can, there's such a thing as "thou protest too much" ... What was that Michael was saying about how he would like to hang the bastards with his "very own" hands? ... *JESUS!* Just as well he didn't get near the Guilford Four, wasn't it?

(We hear the front door opening and shutting and someone approaching.)

COLIN: *(As though alerting DAMIEN)* That'll be Brian ... He's late.

DAMIEN: Big deal.

(BRIAN enters.)

COLIN: You're late ...
BRIAN: *(Glancing at his watch)* Yeah, fuck it ... And I've somewhere to go.
COLIN: You should have used ...
BRIAN: *(Cuts him off. He changes into a shirt, jacket and tie)* Don't tell me, Colin ... "Public Transport" ... And I've missed me sodding dinner.
COLIN: All I was going to say ...
BRIAN: *(Cuts him off again)* I know what you were going to say, Colin ... And, as usual, it would 'ave been a load of bollox ...
COLIN: *(Is embarrassed, but putting a brave face on it, he addresses his next comment to DAMIEN)* Did you know that Brian was clairvoyant, Damien?
BRIAN: *(Sitting down)* "Clair" wot?
COLIN: Clairvoyant ... It means ...
BRIAN: *(Snaps)* I know what it means ... What I'm objecting to is the suggestion that I'd have to be clairvoyant to be able to know that what you were going to say was load of crap ... alright?
COLIN: *(A bit startled by BRIAN's tone)* Alright, alright ... keep your hair on ... I was only ...
BRIAN: I know what you "was only" ... You was only going to launch into one of your bleeding lectures ... Did it ever occur to you that that bomb this morning might 'ave 'ad an effect on the traffic?
COLIN: *(Subdued)* Oh, that ... Do you come that way, then?

BRIAN: Yeah.

COLIN: Could you not have avoided it?

BRIAN: Would I have been late if I could ... Besides, I'm not going to let a crowd of bastards like that dictate to me 'ow to travel around my own, bleeding city.

COLIN: We don't know who did it ... Nobody's claimed it yet.

BRIAN: Who's "we"? ... I bloody do ... *(Turns towards DAMIEN)* Don't you, Damien?

DAMIEN: Oh aye ... the IRA.

BRIAN: *(Eyeing DAMIEN, who remains ice-cool)* Must make you a bit 'omesick ... this bombing and that ...

DAMIEN: There's a few things make me a bit sick here, Brian.

BRIAN: Oh, yeah?

COLIN: *(Attempts to diffuse the situation)* The Guinness for one ... They say it's not a patch on the stuff in Ireland.

DAMIEN: Couldn't tell you, Colin ... Never touch it ...

BRIAN: *(Ignores COLIN's efforts. Continues)* No, I mean like ... well, we 'ave a bomb here and it throws us ... Now I suppose in Belfast you lot would sort of take it in your stride, like ...

DAMIEN: Oh they throw people in Belfast too, Brian ... Considerable distances sometimes ...

COLIN: *(Still trying to fend off tension)* No one was hurt, were they?

BRIAN: You're some baby, Colin ... They can blow the bleeding bollox out of London and as long as nobody's hurt it's alright with you.

COLIN: I didn't say that.

BRIAN: Tell you wot ... I'll go down to your cottage in

the Cotswolds and blow it to fucking bits and as long as "Mummy and Daddy" are out playing Polo, or whatever it is they do, it'll be alright then ... Ok?

COLIN: That's not what I meant.

BRIAN: Wot did you mean then?

COLIN: All I ...

BRIAN: *(Aggressively)* Go on, wot did you mean, wot?

COLIN: *(Annoyed at being bullied)* If you'll only let me ...

BRIAN: Only let you wot?

COLIN: *(Snaps)* Speak.

BRIAN: Speak ...

COLIN: Yes ...

BRIAN: Yes, wot?

COLIN: Yes, let me speak ...

BRIAN: Who's stopping you?

COLIN: *(Turns in frustration to DAMIEN)* Do you believe this?

BRIAN: That ain't speaking ... that's "asking".

COLIN: Because you won't, bloody let me ...

BRIAN: Bullshit ... You 'aven't got anything to say ... that's your problem. You're so full of liberal crap that when guys like the IRA turn up on your own bleeding doorstep you're up shit creek ...

COLIN: I don't believe you, Brian ... In one sentence you've actually employed three different words for "excrement" ...

BRIAN: Yeah, and trust you to come up with a fourth ... and one that don't smell ... to use your own word ... If the "excrement" ever hits the fan here, when the rest of us are fighting, bastards like you'll be writing frigging dictionaries ...

COLIN: Which ... in turn .. bastards like you shall burn, the next time around ...

BRIAN: Too right, ol' son ... only next time we'll throw the wankers who wrote them on as well ...

DAMIEN: Anybody want some tea? No ...

(DAMIEN walks out of the room.)

COLIN: Brian, do you honestly believe ...

BRIAN: *(Watches DAMIEN leave and waits until he is out of earshot)* He didn't 'ave a lot to say for 'isself, did he?

COLIN: What?

BRIAN: About the bombing, like ...

COLIN: I don't quite follow you, Brian ...

BRIAN: Well ... 'im being a Paddy, and all ...

COLIN: What's that got to do with it?

BRIAN: Do me a favour ... Don't you read the papers? *(Tosses the Evening Standard across the table. COLIN looks at the paper)* Don't you see what the cops are saying? ... *(DAMIEN returns. Addresses DAMIEN)* Don't do you a lot of favours, all this ...

DAMIEN: *(Knows what's going on)* What ... you and Colin chewing the balls off each other ... I've got sort of used to it ...

BRIAN: No, not that ... These bombs ...

DAMIEN: I don't get you ...

BRIAN: Well, I mean like, Paddys doing it, an' all.

DAMIEN: Jesus, Brian, you should ring the bomb squad ... seeing as you know their names ...

BRIAN: You're a cool sort of customer, aren't you, Damien ... Clever with it ...

DAMIEN: Oh, I'm clever, Brian ... *(COLIN is getting a bit nervous)* ... That's why I'm sitting here in these shitty digs and working in a shitty job.

BRIAN: That's what I was thinking.

DAMIEN: What were you thinking, Brian?

BRIAN: Well, that a guy like you ... Young, clever ... cool under pressure ... That you wind up in a crap job ... in crap digs ... here in London.

DAMIEN: And what's this "pressure" I'm under?

BRIAN: This bombing, for instance ... Now if I was in Ireland ...

DAMIEN: *(Cuts in)* If you "was" in Ireland your basic training would have taught you how to handle bombing ... and ... you'd have been provided with plenty of back-up ...

BRIAN: You mean as a soldier?

DAMIEN: Is there any other way you'd have been in Ireland?

BRIAN: *(Pauses, stares at DAMIEN)* Is there any other way you'd 'ave been in England?

DAMIEN: What are you saying, Brian?

BRIAN: Like Colin earlier ... I'm not "saying" ... I'm "asking".

COLIN: *(A bit flustered)* Oh, for God's sake ...

BRIAN: *(Cuts COLIN off without looking at him)* Shut it, Colin.

DAMIEN: *(Remains cool, stares at BRIAN)* Well, I did come over once before, ... as a tourist.

BRIAN: *(Realizes that DAMIEN won't be shaken)* Oh, as a tourist. Must have liked it, then?

DAMIEN: It wasn't bad ... Mind you, it's not the same working.

BRIAN: *(Rises from his chair)* I'll bet it's not. *(Looks at his watch)* I'd better be off ... See you later.

COLIN: *(Flustered, uncomfortable)* See you, Brian. *(BRIAN, staring at DAMIEN and ignoring COLIN, exits. Unsure. Apprehensive)* Sorry about that.

DAMIEN: About what? ... Him slagging me about being in the IRA?

COLIN: Yes ... it's his idea of a joke, I'm afraid.

DAMIEN: Colin ... what is it you are afraid of?

COLIN: Nothing ... I just wanted to tell you not to pay attention to him. He has a warped sense of humour.

DAMIEN: *(Unmoved. Cold)* Has he now?

COLIN: Well ... yes. Don't you think so?

DAMIEN: I don't know the bloke long enough to say.

COLIN: Well, I do, and he does.

DAMIEN: And what about that bit he was showing you out of the paper ... The bit where the head of the Anti-Terrorist Squad told people to be on the look-out ... to be vigilant?

COLIN: You don't think Brian was serious, do you?

DAMIEN: I don't see why not. I mean, here we have the top man in the field standing up and appointing the whole, bloody population as vigilantes ... why shouldn't Brian be one of them?

COLIN: *(Getting annoyed)* Oh, for God's sake, Damien, do you honestly believe if that was what he was thinking he would have told you?

DAMIEN: *(Smiles)* Maybe he has a warped sense of humour.

COLIN: Damien ... I've got a meeting at McGrath's this evening. Do you fancy coming for a drink afterwards?

DAMIEN: Yeah, why not ... But it won't be till later, if that's OK ... *(He puts on a stage Irish voice, winks and taps the side of his nose)* ... First oim meeting a few of 'de boyos ... if ye get me drift.

COLIN: Annette would love to meet you ...

DAMIEN: Annette? Ah the girlfriend. I've heard so much about her.

COLIN: You'd like her ...

DAMIEN: Great.

(Lights fade.)

Scene Six

(The pub. Pub sound effects.)

ANNETTE: Does he know hot to get here?

COLIN: Yes ... He'll be here ... Would you like another drink?

ANNETTE: No, this is fine. You sure he knows how to get here?

COLIN: Damien? ... Yeah ... *(Looks at his watch)* It's early yet ... What did you think of the meeting?

ANNETTE: Frustrating ... as usual.

COLIN: You're too impatient ... at least we decided on the bike ride. That was positive.

ANNETTE: It was a compromise ... as soon as the word "occupation" was mentioned the shock-horror reactions from some of them made our stand on nuclear waste look like a round of applause.

COLIN: Occupying a nuclear plant would require an army.

ANNETTE: I was talking about Sellafield. ... All you need to get in there is a bloody ticket ...

COLIN: Anyway ... don't mention it to Damien ...

ANNETTE: Why would I mention it to Damien ... And what if I did?

COLIN: No reason, really ... except ...

ANNETTE: "Except", what?

COLIN: Well he might get the wrong idea.

ANNETTE: Oh, yes?

COLIN: I'm not saying he would ...

ANNETTE: But he could?

COLIN: He might.

ANNETTE: And what exactly might that wrong idea be?

COLIN: I just think it might not be a good idea to mention the occupation.

ANNETTE: What occupation?

COLIN: I know ... But it might sound as though you're trying to make an impression.

ANNETTE: God, Colin there are times when I could *hit* you. *You* are the one who seems to think he's Ireland's answer to Che Guevara.

COLIN: *(Somewhat alarmed)* Whatever you do, don't, for pity's sake, say anything like that when he gets here.

ANNETTE: Why exactly *did* you invite him?

COLIN: That's a funny question ...

ANNETTE: Oh, is it? ... Well what about a funny answer?

COLIN: I thought you'd be curious to meet him, that's all.

ANNETTE: Curious? ... Colin, I don't get the chance to be curious ... Not with you playing Boswell to his Johnson. I thought that maybe you'd invited him for a sort of verbal proof-reading ... You know ... in case you'd got any of the facts about the great man's work wrong ...

COLIN: Annette ...

ANNETTE: ... for instance maybe he's really a Sandanistan leader from Nicaragua and ... as he has to talk through a ski mask, you thought he's said Northern Ireland.

COLIN: *(Glances around. Whispers)* Annette for God's sake ...

ANNETTE: No seriously Colin ... did he say ... *(Stage Irish)* "Up da rebels", or *(Stage Spanish)* "Uppa da Rebele"? You know like Rowan Atkinson when he's doing ...

COLIN: That's not funny ...

ANNETTE: I know that ... and you know that ... but does Rowan Atkinson?

(In the background DAMIEN enters the bar, looking round for COLIN and ANNETTE.)

COLIN: Oh God ... he's here ...

ANNETTE: Where?

COLIN: There by the door ...

ANNETTE: That's never Rowan Atkinson ...

COLIN: Annette please ... God I wish I hadn't asked him.

ANNETTE: Shouldn't he be wearing his ... ?

COLIN: That's it! I'm not asking him over.

ANNETTE: Don't be such a bloody ninny Colin ... besides if you don't I shall.

COLIN: Just promise me, Annette ... When he comes over ...

ANNETTE: Too late ... he's spotted you ... He looks a bit Nicaraguan.

COLIN: Oh God ...

ANNETTE: Should I genuflect?

COLIN: Please, Annette, please. Ah Damien, you found us.

DAMIEN: Well yeah ... you see I sort of had this set of clues to help me.

COLIN: Clues?

DAMIEN: Aye, I sort of figured if I came to the pub you mentioned at around about the time you said, I might just crack it.

COLIN: Oh yes, ha ha, very good.

DAMIEN: So, where's Annette, you said she'd be here.

COLIN: Annette?

ANNETTE: Here, sir. Present.

COLIN: Annette ... of course Annette ... this is Annette ...

DAMIEN: Never!

COLIN: Honest ...

DAMIEN: *(Takes her hand and won't let go)* And what about the beetle-browed hack, ... the scourge of the capitalist press and part-time columnist on Woman's Realm?

COLIN: Struggle, Damien ... "Woman's Struggle" ... It's a paper out ...

DAMIEN: Annette, what can I say ... I'm ...

ANNETTE: Quite a lot it would appear.

DAMIEN: I'm sorry, it's just, well you're not quite what I expected.

ANNETTE: You're not what I expected either.

DAMIEN: Oh?

COLIN: Why don't I get us some ...

ANNETTE: No, I expected you to look more ...

COLIN: Drinks in ...

ANNETTE: Nicaraguan actually.

DAMIEN: Nicaraguan? Before Colin met me he expected me to be more Pakistani ... You English must have a funny way of describing people to each other.

COLIN: Oh yes that, yes that was funny.

(They both look at COLIN.)

DAMIEN: Yes, apparently the whole household had a jolly good laugh over that.

COLIN: No what I mean ...

ANNETTE: You did say something about drinks ...

COLIN: Drinks? Yes, but no-one seemed to be listening.

DAMIEN: What do you expect when you lead me to believe I was to meet Lon Chaney?

COLIN: I'm sure I di ...

ANNETTE: Just get the drinks.

COLIN: He's only .. yes drinks ... Damien?

DAMIEN: Large Bushmills, please.

COLIN: Right. *(Turns to ANNETTE)* And another?

ANNETTE: No. I'll have a ... from what Colin's told you about me, what would you think I'd like?

DAMIEN: From what Colin's told me, ... cocoa ... but having met you ...

ANNETTE: Yes, having met me?

DAMIEN: Well what would you say to a Harvey Wallbanger?

COLIN: Harvey Wallbanger ... I don't think they have them here.

DAMIEN: Jasus, that's a terrible pity Annette, isn't it.

ANNETTE: A sweet sherry please.

COLIN: A sweet ... right ... A Bushmills and a sweet sherry ... and I'll get them in separate glasses *(No reaction)* Right I won't be a tick.

(Leaves)

DAMIEN: Just as well he isn't a policeman. Can you imagine who they'd have lifted when they were chasing John Dillinger if they'd been going on descriptions given by Colin.

ANNETTE: John DeLorean?

DAMIEN: Full marks.

ANNETTE: Oh, I'm being tested.

DAMIEN: Nothing as cerebral as that. I already knew from Colin that you had a great set of brains.

ANNETTE: And that didn't impress you?

DAMIEN: Where I come from brains are ten a penny.

ANNETTE: Oh you have them costed do you? What about arms and legs? How much do they weigh in at?

DAMIEN: Ouch! ... Where did that come from?

ANNETTE: It must be the Lon Chaney in me.

DAMIEN: I must have missed some of his films.

ANNETTE: Pity, he was a hoot.

DAMIEN: I thought you'd have gone for documentaries, you know, with your interest in politics and that.

ANNETTE: What exactly did Colin tell you about me?

DAMIEN: That you're studying journalism. You've a deep and sincere interest in the downtrodden, Social Justice ...

ANNETTE: Deep and sincere interest?

DAMIEN: That's why I didn't spot you when I came in. I was looking for ... well, a nun.

ANNETTE: A nun who looked like Lon Chaney.

DAMIEN: All nuns look like Lon Chaney. Well, to Irish Catholics they do. It's an essential tenet of our faith. The minute you notice that a nun has breasts, you may as well go to Burtons, get yourself a suit and become a Mormon.

ANNETTE: And you noticed that I had tits. It must have come as a shock, Colin not having included that information in my profile.

DAMIEN: Maybe he hasn't noticed.

COLIN: *(Calls from bar)* They only have Jameson's, Damien, will that be alright?

DAMIEN: Yeah, anything.

ANNETTE: Does Colin know that you think he's a twit?

DAMIEN: If that's the impression I gave, it would be wrong. Colin's alright.

ANNETTE: He thinks considerably more of you.

DAMIEN: I assure you that I do nothing to encourage it. It was him who latched onto me. Perhaps because I don't treat him like a twit.

ANNETTE: Which the others at the lodgings do?

DAMIEN: I wouldn't worry about it Annette, he's a big boy now.

ANNETTE: And does he know he's latched onto you? Maybe I should tell him?

DAMIEN: Like the guy in the big picture said Annette "Frankly my dear, I don't give a fuck".

ANNETTE: I'll bet, Damien, that you can be a right bastard.

DAMIEN: For you Annette, anything.

(COLIN returns with the drinks.)

COLIN: Right.

ANNETTE: Damien was just saying that you'd make a terrible policeman.

DAMIEN: Yeah, if we were on the run, it's your descriptions we'd like circulated ...

COLIN: Oh give it a break, you do exaggerate.

ANNETTE: Do you?

DAMIEN: Well yea, I expect Colin's told you about me being a dispatch clerk. Eh Colin?

COLIN: Ah, yeah ...

DAMIEN: Well, I'm really only a warehouse man. Mind you I do make sure that the gear gets to where it has to be.

ANNETTE: I suppose someone has to.

DAMIEN: I think so ... Speaking of what has to be done, how did your meeting go?

ANNETTE: Very well, didn't it, Colin? ... As a matter of fact there's something you might be able to help with.

COLIN: Annette I don't think Damien would be ...

DAMIEN: No hang on Colin, what is it?

ANNETTE: How would you like to help me – us ... organize ... a ... bike ride?

DAMIEN: A bike ride?

ANNETTE: Not your sort of thing Damien.

DAMIEN: Well, I ah ... Where are you going?

COLIN: Going?

DAMIEN: Aye, on your bikes?

ANNETTE: Nowhere.

DAMIEN: Of course, silly me.

COLIN: What she means Damien ...

ANNETTE: I'll let Colin explain. It was his idea ... wasn't it darling?

COLIN: It's not as silly as it sounds. It's a way of drawing attention to ourselves, protesting, lots of groups do it these days.

ANNETTE: Yes lots, I expect there must be lots of bike rides in Ireland, it being so politically active ...

DAMIEN: We're not that advanced. We're still at the hoofing it stage, you know, marching, mind you the Orangemen carry swords.

ANNETTE: That's an idea. What do you think Colin? A sort of bicycle charge ... we could ...

COLIN: Knock it off Annette.

DAMIEN: I think I'll just go to the "jacks".

(Leaves)

COLIN: Annette would you please stop taking the piss out of the bike ride. And you shouldn't have asked Damien about it.

ANNETTE: Not in his league?

COLIN: It's not a matter of leagues, it's just ... well ...

ANNETTE: Pathetic.

COLIN: So why did you go along with it at the meeting?

ANNETTE: I'll tell you why Colin ... I was afraid that if we didn't settle on the bloody bike ride, we'd end up with another letter writing campaign, or organic jam making. Mind you, if Damien really wants to help letter writing it could be upgraded to something with a little more impact ... Like a parcel bomb campaign ...

COLIN: That's seriously not funny.

ANNETTE: Exactly Colin. Don't you ever long to do something that isn't just for "fun", or be something other than "in solidarity with"? God, how many struggles are in we solidarity with? Nicaragua, South Africa, Ireland, El Salvador ...

COLIN: For God's sake Annette ...

ANNETTE: What exactly is our function ... to hold the coats of the people who do the actual struggling? ... And why am I drinking this crap!

COLIN: You bloody well asked for it.

ANNETTE: That's typical of you Colin. You've got this vice-like grip on reality, cold, relentless ... academic with avengence ...

COLIN: And what's that supposed to mean?

ANNETTE: It means *(DAMIEN is approaching)* stop quibbling and get me a ... Harvey Wallbanger, please.

COLIN: I'll go and ask them. Damien do you want another?

DAMIEN: Tell you what, they're going to close here shortly. What would you say to us picking up a carry-out and going back to where we can talk?

COLIN: Well I'm not sure. I was up late last night and ...

DAMIEN: Jasus Colin, at your age, sure that should be no problem ... or is it going back to ... sorry Annette, it was a bit presumptuous ...

ANNETTE: Are you any good at Harvey Wallbangers?

DAMIEN: Wicked. I would've suggested our place, but as you might know, it's a bit of a no-go area for anything other than eating and sleeping. You might describe it as a sort of zoo.

COLIN: Right. Well, I'd better go and pay for the room **for tonight's meeting** ...

ANNETTE: It would never do for the revolution to be evicted from the pub.

COLIN: You know you get funnier and funnier ... I'll meet you outside the off-license.

(Walks off.)

ANNETTE: *(Putting on her coat)* And don't forget to get a receipt.

DAMIEN: Very acidic stuff this sherry ...

ANNETTE: In this "zoo" you live in, what's Colin's role, mother hen?

DAMIEN: Mother hen? That's a funny way to refer to your lover.

ANNETTE: My lover ... Is that what Colin told you?

DAMIEN: He didn't tell me that. It's what he thinks.

ANNETTE: We've known each other since we were about ten and we met at university. And how come you know what he thinks ... especially if he doesn't tell you?

DAMIEN: You can know without being told.

ANNETTE: And what's your role in the "zoo", ringmaster?

DAMIEN: That's not a zoo that's a circus.

ANNETTE: And what's the difference?

DAMIEN: Circuses have safety nets.

ANNETTE: What?

(They leave. Fade lights.)

Scene Seven

(Cross fade lighting to ANNETTE's flat. About an hour later.

COLIN has keeled over on the sofa and is sleeping. ANNETTE is sitting at the other end of the same sofa. DAMIEN is sitting at the table.)

DAMIEN: He wasn't kidding when he said he was knackered, was he?

(Nods towards COLIN.)

ANNETTE: *(Lifting her glass)* Not to mention this stuff ... He doesn't drink much.
DAMIEN: It was my fault really ... I was a bit pushy about the carryout.
ANNETTE: He could have said no ...
DAMIEN: You reckon ... ?
ANNETTE: *(A bit bemused)* What do you mean?
DAMIEN: Ah, nothing ... *(Rises with the bottle and approaches her)* Here, have a top up.
ANNETTE: No, I'm curious ... What did you mean?
DAMIEN: Well, it's his nature, isn't it ... he's too kind ... too good mannered.
ANNETTE: *(Fishing)* You think so?
DAMIEN: Yeah, for his own good ... He didn't want to let anybody down ... Spoil the fun.
ANNETTE: Do you like him?
DAMIEN: Yeah, ... He's a nice bloke.
ANNETTE: Yes, but what do you *think* of him?
DAMIEN: *(Becomes wary)* I thought I just answered that.

(Returns to sit.)

ANNETTE: You did and you didn't ... I like carrots but if you asked me what I thought about them, I'd say "bugger all".

DAMIEN: *(A little exasperated)* Annette, I have the feeling that I'm being cross-questioned in pursuit of some end I'm not aware of ...

ANNETTE: That's called paranoia, Damien.

DAMIEN: I know what it's called, Annette. Fear of heights is called vertigo but you don't get it until you're on the edge of a cliff ...

ANNETTE: You feel you're on the edge of a cliff?

DAMIEN: I feel I'm on the edge of something ... What's all this about Colin ... one minute you're taking the piss out of him and the next ... well with me anyway ... you seem to be sort of protecting him ... From what ... *me*?

ANNETTE: *(She holds out her glass)* Here ... Refill, please.

DAMIEN: *(He does so)* Yes?

ANNETTE: Since he's met you ... *(Pause)* he's changed ... For the better in many ways. It's like he's on a sort of "high". He's more positive ... enthusiastic ... more full of life.

DAMIEN: *(Unsure how to react)* Ummmm ... That doesn't sound too bad.

ANNETTE: It isn't ... in itself.

DAMIEN: So ... What's the other side of the coin?

ANNETTE: *(Turns and looks at COLIN)* Look at him ... that's Colin ... a cuddly, good-hearted, loving ... human being.

(She's struggling for expression and stops.)

DAMIEN: *(Waits for a time. Almost whispers)* Yes.

ANNETTE: *(More composed and without looking at DAMIEN)* That zoo you live in ... If he strays too far into it ... it'll devour him ...

(Looks straight at DAMIEN.)

DAMIEN: *(Quietly)* Then, Annette ... why don't you take him out of it?

ANNETTE: *(Surprised)* Ha! ... therein lies the rub ...

(Pauses)

DAMIEN: *(Gently)* I know.

ANNETTE: I expect *you* do.

DAMIEN: It's because of you he's there.

ANNETTE: *(Affectionately)* Full marks, Mister clever clogs.

DAMIEN: I knew it the minute I saw him ... "There" ... I says to meself ... "is a Dilemma Devil".

ANNETTE: A what?

DAMIEN: A "Dilemma Devil"? ... Someone who seems to thrive on the horns of a dilemma, sort of hooked ... there's another word for it.

ANNETTE: *(Wary)* And what word would that be?

DAMIEN: The one that sticks in your throat.

ANNETTE: *(Tense)* Say it.

DAMIEN: *(Looking steadily at ANNETTE)* A loser.

ANNETTE: That's a cruel thing to say?

DAMIEN: Is it? ... Is it cruel to observe it, think it ... or just to say it. Do you think that I am cruel?

ANNETTE: I don't know ... I ... expect you ... could be ...

DAMIEN: Do you want me to leave?

ANNETTE: *(Staring at him)* No ...

DAMIEN: You're very gracious ... when we finish this bottle I'll hit the road.

ANNETTE: *(Still staring at him)* He told me about you.

DAMIEN: He doesn't know anything about me to tell.

ANNETTE: Aren't you afraid that he knows ... and that he told me?

DAMIEN: And what does he know?

ANNETTE: That you're politically involved.

DAMIEN: Colin hasn't seen me with as much as a leaflet.

ANNETTE: I'm sure of that.

DAMIEN: *(Small laugh)* And what's that supposed to mean?

ANNETTE: I wouldn't think you'd be on the ballot box end of things.

DAMIEN: Oh, wouldn't you?

ANNETTE: No.

DAMIEN: So ... what do *you* think I am?

ANNETTE: I don't know.

DAMIEN: Well everything's fine then, isn't it?

ANNETTE: Don't patronize me.

DAMIEN: And don't you be talking to me about things you know nothing about.

ANNETTE: I'm not Colin ... He's a romantic ... when he sees suffering ... injustice ... it hurts him and he feels he *has* to do something about it ... The problem is he can't because he can't take the pain ...

DAMIEN: What pain?

ANNETTE: The pain involved in really doing something about it. He thinks living in that horrible house is in some way a "statement" and, like you said, to "impress" me. The problem is, the more I tell him he should get out, the greater he thinks his "statement" ... his pseudo-struggle ... is. He ...

DAMIEN: Annette ... why are you telling me all this?

ANNETTE: Do you know, I'm not quite sure.

DAMIEN: Are you afraid I'll put you in the same boat as Colin?

ANNETTE: *(Flares)* You arrogant bastard.

DAMIEN: Jesus, arrogant now ... First it was cruel, now it's arrogant. I'm telling you, if they ever make a film about me they'll have to revive Hammer Studios and resuscitate Vincent Price to do the part.

ANNETTE: OK I over-reacted ... But you really *are* an arrogant bastard.

DAMIEN: I suppose I am ... a bit.

ANNETTE: *(Laughs)* You are something else ... tell me, what would this film be about?

DAMIEN: Well let me see ... How about "The Life And Times Of The Man Who Threw Off The Yoke Of British Imperialism In Ireland By Going Over And Blowing The Living Bejasus Out Of England" ... *(He looks at ANNETTE who is taken aback and makes no response)* You don't like the title ... Too long?

ANNETTE: Isn't that rather a dangerous thing to say?

DAMIEN: *(Suddenly very serious)* It depends upon who you say it to.

ANNETTE: So why did you say it to me?

DAMIEN: Because I knew you could take a joke.

ANNETTE: Some joke.

DAMIEN: Yeah, I know ... It's had us in stitches in Ireland for over three hundred years. *(He drains his glass and stands up)* Well, that's the end of the whisky ... I'll be hitting the road ... Thanks again for your hospitality. *(He stands over her head and hands her his empty glass. She doesn't get up)* Shall I be seeing you again?

ANNETTE: Yes.

(Blackout)

ACT II

Scene One

(The dining room. The 'phone rings. DAMIEN answers it. ANNETTE is on another 'phone in another part of the set.)

DAMIEN: Hello ...

ANNETTE: Damien, I'm glad it's you.

DAMIEN: Annette? ... Hold on a minute and I'll go and get Colin ... I think he might be in the ...

ANNETTE: *(Quickly)* No ... no, Damien ... It's you I wanted to talk to ...

DAMIEN: Oh yeah?

ANNETTE: Is Colin there?

DAMIEN: I think he's in the bath ... Why?

ANNETTE: Ah ... this is a bit awkward. *(Pause)* isn't it?

DAMIEN: *(After a time)* What's a bit awkward, Annette?

ANNETTE: This ...

DAMIEN: *(Realizes, smiles)* God, I'd have thought that an educated woman like yourself would have been well used to 'phones by now ...

ANNETTE: Very amusing ... You know what I mean ... The point is, I'd like to talk to you ...

DAMIEN: Ok ... I wanted to talk to you too.

ANNETTE: Not on the 'phone, you idiot.

DAMIEN: Meet you for a drink?
ANNETTE: No, not the pub ... But I do have a bottle of Bushmills in the flat.
DAMIEN: I see ... your flat?
ANNETTE: Well you can't really talk in a pub ...
DAMIEN: Yeah ... I know what you mean ... I won't mention it, I take it ...
ANNETTE: It's about what you were saying the other night ... It's got nothing really to do with Colin.
DAMIEN: And what was I saying the other night?
ANNETTE: We'll talk about it when you get here ... Nine o'clock suit you?
DAMIEN: Yeah, that'll be dead-on ...
COLIN: *(Off)* Oh, Damien, it was for you.

(We hear/see COLIN approaching.)

DAMIEN: Yeah ... Bye ...
ANNETTE: See you then.

(Hangs up.)

COLIN: I thought it might have been Annette.
DAMIEN: *(With discomfort, guilt)* Yes. No.
COLIN: Everything alright?
DAMIEN: Oh yea. You know phone calls and that ... you know ...
COLIN: Oh, I see.
DAMIEN: Well ... it's bad enough being a Paddy as it is, but there's times when you listen to the news and you'd think it was a hanging offense.

COLIN: You don't have to explain to me, Damien. We're not all like Brian you know.

DAMIEN: Thank Christ for that. Can you imagine the crap he'd come out with he took a call from Belfast.

COLIN: Was that where ... ? *(Puts his hands to his mouth)* Shit ... sorry ... I wasn't ...

DAMIEN: It's OK. Relax ...

COLIN: I know exactly what you mean ... Annette's phoned me a few times and Brian's taken them ... You can just imagine the meal he made out of that.

DAMIEN: Beats me why you don't just give him a kick in the bollocks ...

COLIN: *(Smiles)* Yea ... *(Glances at watch)* Anyway, I'd better give Annette a ring ... I've a video of an absolutely brilliant film ...

DAMIEN: *(Face into cup)* Yeah?

COLIN: *(On the way out)* Yeah, "La Belle et La Bete".

DAMIEN: La what et la what?

COLIN: Cocteau's "Beauty and the Beast".

(DAMIEN remains at the table. COLIN goes to the 'phone. He dials.)

DAMIEN: *(Groans)* Shit.

COLIN: Hi, it's me. I got it ... the video. La belle et la bete ... Shall I bring it over, I can't wait to see it, ... what? ... Oh ... well ... c'est la vie, ... yeah well I'll ring you tomorrow. Night night, sleep tight. *(He hangs up, goes and sits at the table)* Bugger ...

DAMIEN: Problems?

COLIN: Yeah ... her bloody mother's over.

DAMIEN: So that's the film knocked on the head, is it?

COLIN: Ironic isn't it? ... Took me weeks to get Cocteau's "Beauty and the Beast" and now, if I had a video camera, I could go round there and film my own bloody version ... anyway can't be helped ... What about you and me going out for a few beers? I don't fancy that room tonight.

DAMIEN: Can't, sorry ... I've ...

COLIN: Somewhere to go ... Never mind ... *(DAMIEN just stares at him. After a short pause, COLIN realizes)* Good for you! Sorry, Damien ... that must have sounded dreadful, sorry.

DAMIEN: *(Irritated)* Alright, Alright ... you've nothing to be sorry for. *(Pause)* I didn't mean to snap, Colin ... I ...

COLIN: No, it's OK. I ...

(DAMIEN holds his hand up to stop him speaking and walks off.)
(Lights fade.)

Scene Two

(The lights go up on a scene in the bedroom. MICHAEL is lying on the bed reading a newspaper. BRIAN enters. He is dressed as though just having had a night out.)

MICHAEL: *(Looking up at BRIAN's entrance)* Brian ... How goes it?

BRIAN: Michael ... been down the Pub?

MICHAEL: Aye ... It was bloody packed the night ...

BRIAN: Michael, does Damien ever get down there?

MICHAEL: Not that I've seen ... I don't think he bothers too much with the gargle.

BRIAN: No ... I didn't think he would.

MICHAEL: Why's that?

BRIAN: Well ... 'ee's too clever, ain't 'ee.

MICHAEL: What's so bloody clever about him? ... He's a cocky bastard, I'll hand you that.

BRIAN: What do you think of 'im?

MICHAEL: Like I said, he's a cocky bastard ...

BRIAN: Yeah ... but what do you think 'ee's up to?

MICHAEL: *(Realizes that BRIAN is more than casual)* What do you mean "up to"?

BRIAN: Well, this "shift" work, and that ...

MICHAEL: So he's on shift work ... so what?

BRIAN: Sort of 'andy "shift work", ain't it ... I mean, like it covers an awful lot ...

MICHAEL: *(Doesn't follow him)* "Covers" you for what?

BRIAN: Coming and going, like ... You know, at odd hours.

MICHAEL: That's why it's called "shift" work.

BRIAN: Yeah ... But what's 'ee shifting?

MICHAEL: Brian, what ... in God's name ... are you getting at?

(We hear the front doorbell going in the distance.)

BRIAN: Don't you ever read the papers?

MICHAEL: *(Puzzled)* "The papers"?

BRIAN: *(Lifts the paper MICHAEL has discarded)* You know ... these big white things with lots of squiggly little black marks and lines all over them ...

MICHAEL: Oh them ... I thought they were for wiping your arse with ...

BRIAN: Maybe where you come from ... Over 'ere we read 'em first ...

MICHAEL: And then have fish and chips in them ... and then you wipe your arse with them ... which would go a long way in explaining why you're such a slippery shower of bastards.

BRIAN: Come off it, Michael ... you know you love it over 'ere. Not like some I could mention ...

MICHAEL: *(Narrowing his eyes)* Are you saying what I think you're saying?

BRIAN: Put it this way, Michael ... If I was looking for you I'd put out a poster ... or whatever ... saying ... "Have you seen a middle-aged Irishman ... five foot ten ... balding ... blue eyes? Always smiling, I might add. Right? Now isn't that what I'd do?

MICHAEL: *(Cautious)* Yeeess ...

BRIAN: But it don't always work out like that, do it? ... There's a description of a bloke in the paper who's being looked for ... A number of 'em, actually. "Are you suspicious of anyone? Possibly a neighbor? Irish accent ..."

MICHAEL: *(Is dismissive, but also a little uneasy)* That could be half a million bloody people.

BRIAN: Exactly ... But it ain't, is it? ... It' some-bloody-body ... A real person ... who plants real bombs ...

MICHAEL: *(A little uncomfortable)* I know that, but ...

BRIAN: "But" nothing ... like you said, it could be anybody. That's the beauty of it. Because of that nobody bothers looking ...

(Watches MICHAEL.)

MICHAEL: *(The strain growing)* What?

BRIAN: Come off it, Michael ... Do we know anybody who fits this description ... or non-description? Do we?

MICHAEL: You're just imagining things.

BRIAN: 'Ee's the right age ... 'ee's bright ... It weren't no thick Paddys in Brighton who slipped that bomb into Margaret Thatcher's hotel, now were it?

MICHAEL: *(Can't help himself, but is still nervous)* Just goes to show how far a Paddy has to go to get a bit of respect in this Country ...

BRIAN: *(Stone cold reaction)* Or ... thirty bleeding years ...

MICHAEL: *(Tries to break the tension)* Ah, for Christsake, Brian ... knock it off, will ya ...

(We hear footsteps on the stairs, then MRS. SOMERS calling out.)

MRS. SOMERS: *(Off)* Damien ...

MICHAEL: He's not here.

MRS. SOMERS: *(Who unbeknownst to MICHAEL is already standing in the doorway)* You don't 'ave to shout, lad ... I'm not deaf ... *(She is carrying a parcel)* A lad dropped this off for Damien ...

(Goes towards DAMIEN's bed.)

BRIAN: *(Reaches for parcel.)* Is it ticking?
MRS. SOMERS: *(Holds the parcel close into herself)*

Silly bugger. You just keep your nose where it belongs ... between your shifty little cockney eyes ...

BRIAN: That's why I want to know if it's ticking ... I want "everything" I 'ave to stay where it belongs ... And all in one piece ...

MRS. SOMERS: What are you gibbering about?

MICHAEL: Ach, pay no heed to him ... He's been like that since he came in ...

MRS. SOMERS: Aye, Michael ... but what's 'ee getting at?

BRIAN: 'ow much do you know about this Damien geezer? ... that's what I'm getting at ...

MRS. SOMERS: 'ow much do I know about you? ... And Brian, lad ... I've heard you at table and I think you're getting a bit out of hand ... now you and Michael rib each other ... And as for poor Colin ... I don't know how the lad can stand it ... but Damien, 'ee's a different kettle of fish ...

BRIAN: *(Disparaging laugh)* You can say that again, Darling ...

MRS. SOMERS: *(Continues as though not interrupted)* And you can't 'andle 'im ...

BRIAN: *(Incensed)* Wot's to bleeding 'andle?

MRS. SOMERS: You tell me, lad ... It's you as is going on about 'im.

MICHAEL: *(Trying to ease things)* Well, you have to admit ... he doesn't exactly "mix in" ...

MRS. SOMERS: Wi' what, Michael? ... silly bugger talk at table ... or supping ale wi' you in pub ... The lad's out after lassies ... something the pair of you should 'ave put more time into when you were his age.

BRIAN: *(Thrusts out the newspaper showing her a*

headline about a bombing) What about "that"?

MRS. SOMERS: *(Squints to look at paper)* Grow up Brian!

(Exits, having left the parcel on the bed.)
(Lights Fade.)

Scene Three

(The dining room. It is the early hours of the morning, MRS. SOMERS is sitting snoozing in her chair, an open paper in her lap. She starts awake. She looks at her watch.)

MRS. SOMERS: What am I Jack ... half daft or what ... *(We hear a noise at the front door. She goes back to her chair. DAMIEN puts his head round the door)* Damien.

DAMIEN: Jasus, Mrs. Somers. Bloody hell, you put the heart across me. I didn't see you there, sorry. What's up?

MRS. SOMERS: I wanted a word with you.

DAMIEN: You didn't have to ambush me.

MRS. SOMERS: Ever the clever one ... I didn't know I'd be here til now. I fell asleep. Do you usually get in at this hour?

DAMIEN: Sometimes I get in late.

MRS. SOMERS: You're full of yourself, wiping some poor lasses eye wi' that blarney of yours, eh?

DAMIEN: I'm in love Mrs. Somers.

MRS. SOMERS: Aye, and it sounds like you like her too. Well you can drop anchor for a minute. I want a word.

DAMIEN: Oh dear, sounds ominous.

MRS. SOMERS: Naught ominous about it, lad.

DAMIEN: Well, what's up?

MRS. SOMERS: You tell me ... The last few weeks there's been an atmosphere in here you could cut with a knife.

DAMIEN: Atmosphere?

MRS. SOMERS: It's not an elocution lesson, Damien. You don't have to repeat everything I say.

DAMIEN: What atmosphere?

MRS. SOMERS: The one around this table at times ... *and* I can hear the lot of you in that room when you get going.

DAMIEN: What? The banter between me and Brian?

MRS. SOMERS: Aye ... *and* Michael ... And God alone knows what's got into Colin this past while.

DAMIEN: And all this is down to me?

MRS. SOMERS: Well it's not down to anything I'm putting in food, is it? You're just not getting along wi' the other lads, isn't that it?

DAMIEN: It depends on what you mean by "getting along" ... I'll tell you something I'm not ... I'm not "going" along ... But then, is there any law that says I have to?

MRS. SOMERS: Not as you'd call a law ... But is there any point if you're not?

DAMIEN: Oh, I see ... perhaps you think I should leave ...

MRS. SOMERS: That's not what I'm saying, lad. If it were you wouldn't mistake it. No, I'm curious more than anything else ... Besides, where would you move to ... next door ... next street? ... wherever it was, it would be much the same.

DAMIEN: I'm not complaining, Mrs. Somers.

MRS. SOMERS: Not complaining, I know that, lad ...

You're enjoying it, from what I can see ... But there's other things to be taken into consideration.

DAMIEN: Oh aye?

MRS. SOMERS: You've heard expression ... "an Englishman's home is his castle"?

DAMIEN: I have indeed, Mrs. Somers ... Often.

MRS. SOMERS: Well this Englishwoman's home is also her living ...

DAMIEN: And I'm a disruptive influence?

MRS. SOMERS: "Disruptive"? ... For one thing you've Michael running 'round like he were head of Klu Klux Klan and ...

DAMIEN: Sometimes I think he is.

MRS. SOMERS: Aye, be that as it may ... he never used to.

DAMIEN: Before I came?

MRS. SOMERS: Aye, lad ... Whatever nonsense he had in his head used to stay there ... for the most part not any more ... I'm afraid to put wireless on in morning now in case there's a mention of cricket on it and the Pakistanis are winning ... or losing, come to that, and he starts ranting and raving. In all the years he's been here I've never had to tell him to shut up as much as I've had to this past six or seven weeks.

DAMIEN: It wasn't me put it there to come out, Mrs. Somers.

MRS. SOMERS: Aye, but have you heard of cans of worms ... or, as Colin might put it ... Pandora's Box ... There's things that are as well left alone, and the contents of Michael Connelly's head is one of 'em.

DAMIEN: It was him started on to me. The very first morning I was here he was at it. Michael has his own version of "How to make Friends and Influence People" ... What it boiled down to was join the National Front.

MRS. SOMERS: Maybe that was just how you chose to take it?

DAMIEN: At the risk of sounding funny, Mrs. Somers, he made it pretty black and white. What was I supposed to do ... Go along with it?

MRS. SOMERS: You could have ignored it.

DAMIEN: Sure ... I could have cut a couple of holes out of one of your pillowcases and pulled it over me head ... That would have kept him happy ... and quiet, I suppose.

MRS. SOMERS: That's your problem, Damien ... You takes things to extremes ... Instead of telling him what a silly bugger he were, you went and whipped him into a lather ... and now it's my problem too ... But Michael's the least of it. What about Brian?

DAMIEN: Brian? What about him?

MRS. SOMERS: Well it's not coloured folk that you have him climbing the walls about, is it?

DAMIEN: Mrs. Somers, maybe you haven't noticed ... the chances are you don't care ... but Brian is a total bigot ... Me just being here is enough to send him up the walls.

MRS. SOMERS: Why, ... 'cause you're Irish?

DAMIEN: So you've noticed too.

MRS. SOMERS: *(Sharp)* Don't come all sarky wi' me, lad ... It's nought to do wi' you being Irish. Michael's Irish and the pair of them seem to manage.

DAMIEN: If I'm being sarcastic it's because I feel in a rather perverse situation, sat down like a naughty schoolboy and ticked off for not caving in to the local bullies.

MRS. SOMERS: That's your only concern, isn't it ...

You not caving in ... The thing is, lad ... Have you any idea where it might lead you?

DAMIEN: That seems clear enough ... out on the street.

MRS. SOMERS: It might be more a question of "inside" than out ... Do you know what notions you've put in Brian's head?

DAMIEN: Whatever they are, are you telling me that he talked to you about them?

MRS. SOMERS: Given what they are ... and this being my home ... he were entitled to ... *(Pause)* He thinks you might be one of those who's been planting bombs.

DAMIEN: *(Coolly)* Does he now ... and what makes him think that?

MRS. SOMERS: You tell me, lad.

DAMIEN: Do you think I am?

MRS. SOMERS: I very much doubt it. But you seem to go out of your way to keep Brian on tenterhooks about the whole thing.

DAMIEN: What "whole thing"?

MRS. SOMERS: You know well what "whole thing" ... I've listened to you at table ... You won't give an inch ... If Brian says aught about bombing or like, you sit back, cool as a cucumber and watch him get 'isself in a state while you play wi' him like a cat wi' a mouse. I'm not saying you go along wi' it but you make damn sure you don't go agin it ... I know it's a game, lad ... but it's a dangerous one ... and like they say ... there could be tears before nightfall ...

DAMIEN: And what if it's not ... Well, not *just* a game?

MRS. SOMERS: You and lads bombing, you reckon?

DAMIEN: It's got nothing to do with the lads bombing ... The only bombing I'm concerned with is the bombing Brian's into.

MRS. SOMERS: And what bombing would that be?

DAMIEN: Take a look at one of his casualties, Michael, and you just might see what I mean. The man's totally emasculated ... You've heard *his* reaction when a bomb goes off ... he wants to be at the head of the mob who kick them to death ...

MRS. SOMERS: Oh, aye ... And where would you want to be?

DAMIEN: Well what about ... at their trial ... but you've missed the most important point. Not only is he a more than willing volunteer for the mob, he wants to be seen as its most ardent member ... Now that, Mrs. Somers, has got nothing whatsoever to do with conviction ... and *everything* to do with a perverted sense of guilt born out of repression ... The sort of day-in-day-out repression practiced by Brian and the tens of thousands of wee Brians running all over this Country ... not to mention the more moronic elements of the press who fuel the situation.

MRS. SOMERS: And what does that grand mouthful mean ... You agree wi' the bombing of innocent men, women and children?

DAMIEN: I'll tell you what it means, Mrs. Somers ... Like you pointed out earlier, when you said I always refused to go against the bombers ... It means I refuse to answer the question, "Have you stopped beating your wife?"

MRS. SOMERS: Which means?

DAMIEN: It means ... The only time I ever hear Ireland mentioned in this Country is when some guy blows a wee bit of it up. And then the only question is how the hell he managed it – Not why the Hell he bothered in the first place. And when the question is aimed at me it's not from the point of view, "Oh, you're Irish, can you help cast any light on this?" No. It just boils down to "Are you with us or against us?" ... I'll tell you something else, if the people asking were willing to cast a wee bit of light on why I was born and reared looking down the barrel of a British gun in *my* country, I might be prepared to co-operate.

MRS. SOMERS: Why can't you say all this to Brian?

DAMIEN: I would if it could be translated into "Sun-speak". Besides ... you know these guys running 'round planting bombs ... that's what they're doing ... addressing the whole thing at the level the Brians of this Country insist on keeping it. You ask Brian what he know about the situation in Ireland and he'll have no hesitation in telling you that he knows sweet FA about it. It doesn't stop him telling you what the solution to it is, though. And I'm supposed to sit nodding at him like a toy dog over my cornflakes when he brings up what a shower of bastards the IRA are ... *(Stands to go)* Well, if you'll excuse the language, Mrs. Somers, I won't lick arse. One Paddy in this house licking his arse is full quota, so the next time he comes whinging to you, you can tell him that.

MRS. SOMERS: It might not be me he goes whinging to, the next time.

DAMIEN: *(Goes to the door)* He can please himself ... and I'll leave if you want me to ... There's nothing to keep me ... nothing to keep me here ... At the moment I don't give ...

MRS. SOMERS: Do you, Damien? Do you support them?

DAMIEN: *(Stops at door and turns. Considers a moment)* I can't answer that question ... Won't, rather ... Not under these conditions.

MRS. SOMERS: What conditions?

DAMIEN: I read a poem once. It was written by a black man, he was part of the first wave of immigrants into this Country. He came believing all the "Mothercountry" bullshit. Do you know what his poem was about? The narrative, the story, of the poem was about him working on the London Underground and hearing of a bad train crash, and what flashed through his mind when he heard ... and do you know what that was? ... "God, please let the driver not be a black man". The poem was about guilt and shame. The fact that the train crash had nothing to do with him was neither here nor there ... You see he needed an alibi for his whole people before it was any good. So you see, Mrs. Somers, it's not that I have any difficulty with the question, it's just being asked it that bugs.

(Lights fade.)

Scene Four

(DAMIEN and COLIN are in their room. Each is occupied in their own activity, It is 7 PM. BRIAN enters.)

BRIAN: *(As he enters, he encounters COLIN first, who looks up)* ... There's somebody on the phone downstairs.
COLIN: *(Jumping up)* Oh, good ...

(As he rushes across the room ... BRIAN turns to watch him.)

BRIAN: *(Just as COLIN reaches the door)* Who said it was for you?

COLIN: *(Retreats from the door-way)* You said ... I thought ...

BRIAN: I said there was someone on the phone ... I didn't say that it was for you, mate ... *(Turns to DAMIEN)* ... It's for you, Damien ... That posh bird ... "again" ...

DAMIEN: *(Gets up and exits past COLIN, who is still standing)* Right ... thanks.

BRIAN: *(After DAMIEN's left)* 'ee's doing alright for 'imself, ... 'ain't 'ee?

COLIN: *(Returns to his work)* What?

BRIAN: Your mate ... The member for West Belfast ... 'ee's doing alright for 'is-self ...

COLIN: *(Not interested in BRIAN's banter)* Listen, Brian ... I'm ... trying to get on with some work, here.

BRIAN: Oh, don't let me stop you.

COLIN: Thanks ... It's just that I want this finished for the ... morning.

BRIAN: You carry on, me ol' mate ... *(Pauses and then continues)* ... Just as well then, innit ...

COLIN: *(A little exasperated)* What is?

BRIAN: That that call weren't for you ... Wot, with all that ... work to do, an all.

COLIN: It's just that I thought it might have been my mother.

BRIAN: 'ere, that's a thought ... She 'as a posh accent, hasn't she ... No ... What am I on about ... If it 'ad been your mum she wouldn't 'ave asked for Damien, now would she ...

COLIN: Hardly ...

(Tries to return to his work.)

BRIAN: Of course not ... Funny 'ow I forgot about that for a minute ... 'er asking for Damien, I mean ... And it's not the sort of name you forget, is it?

COLIN: No.

BRIAN: I mean, bleeding, Damien ... Where do they get 'em from. It likely means something in Paddy language ... You know ... "Oak-Tree" ... or ... "Cow-Pat" ... Something like that.

COLIN: Brian, I'm not in the mood for your so-called wit tonight ... So, if you don't mind ...

(Returns to work.)

BRIAN: Oh ... I do beg your pardon ... We are in a mood tonight, aren't we ...

COLIN: *(Without lifting his head)* Yes, Brian, we are.

BRIAN: *(Lying back on his bed)* Ooh ... pardon me for breathing. *(They fall into silence, COLIN keeping his head bent to his papers, BRIAN glancing over at him once in a while.) (As though talking to himself)* It's just that these ... posh voices all sound the same to me ... *(After a pause, BRIAN lifts his hand as though talking into a telephone. He puts on a mock female "posh" accent)* "Hello ... I say ... is Damien there"?

COLIN: *(Exasperated)* Brian ... Do you mind?

BRIAN: Sorry, I didn't know you were listening ... it's just been since you've come here, y'know ... *(He repeats the telephone routing)* "Hello ... is Colin there"? *(Returns to normal voice)* If it's not your mother it's one of your sisters ... *(He pauses and puts his hands back behind his head)* Or that other one ... wot's 'er name ... "Annette" ...

COLIN: *(Jumps up and begins to gather his papers)* That's it, I'm ...

BRIAN: *(Jumps up into a sitting position on the side of the bed)* OK, OK ... I'll pack it in ... I was just trying to be bleeding 'elpful ...

COLIN: Is that what you were doing?

(Just then DAMIEN enters.)

BRIAN: Damien ... You try and explain something to 'im and 'ee gets the bleeding hump ...

DAMIEN: Oh aye? ...

(He glances at COLIN who avoids looking at him.)

BRIAN: Yeah ... I was just telling 'im how I can't tell the difference between one posh voice and another.

COLIN: Oh, for God's sake, shut up, Brian.

BRIAN: *(To DAMIEN)* Can you?

COLIN: *(Jumps up and storms out of the room)* Fuck you ... Fuck you ...

BRIAN: *(Mock astonishment)* Gor blimey ... 'ou did 'ee say that to ... You or me?

DAMIEN: *(Turns on BRIAN)* I suppose you've been tormenting him ... since I've been out of the room.

BRIAN: *(Is suddenly very cool and collected. He stares at DAMIEN for some time and talks in a slow, deliberate fashion)* Me ... Are you asking me ... if I'm tormenting 'im?

DAMIEN: What's the matter ... Can you not understand my accent either?

BRIAN: Oh, I can understand it alright ... You see, now-a-days, in this Country you 'ave to be sort of "multi-lingual".

DAMIEN: So you told him, did you?

BRIAN: *(Mock bewilderment)* "Told 'im"? ... Told 'im what?

DAMIEN: You know damned well.

BRIAN: *(Mock "sudden enlightenment")* Oh ... that ... That you're ... fucking Annette.

DAMIEN: You ...

(He rushes towards BRIAN but is brought to a sudden halt when BRIAN produces a knife.)

BRIAN: You were saying ...

DAMIEN: I might have guessed ...

BRIAN: Wot might you 'ave guessed?

DAMIEN: That you'd be the sort of wee shite who'd carry a knife.

BRIAN: And wot's wrong with that ... Are you one of these pacifists?

DAMIEN: *(Watching the knife)* Put the knife away ...

BRIAN: Does the sight of weapons offend you?

DAMIEN: Only when they're pointing at me.

BRIAN: I thought so.

DAMIEN: One of these days I'm going to break your fucking neck.

BRIAN: Oh yeah, ... you and who's army.

DAMIEN: Brian ... what exactly have you got ... in that puddle of shit you call a brain?

BRIAN: I'm fucking telling you ... *(DAMIEN walks right up to within an inch of the knife which is now shaking. He stands staring into BRIAN's eyes for a moment. DAMIEN turns and exits slowly. Deliberately. BRIAN sits on his bed, almost weeping) (Muttering)* We'll see ... we'll fucking see.

(Lights fade.)

Scene Five

(ANNETTE's flat. She is finishing dressing [make-up, whatever] her entryphone rings. As she goes to answer it she looks a little puzzled and glances at her wrist-watch.)

ANNETTE: *(Surprised)* Colin ... Come on up. *(Hangs up)* Fuck it. Shit.

(S*he opens the door, COLIN is there.)*

COLIN: *(Entering)* Surprise ...
ANNETTE: *(Having "collected" herself)* Yes ... Yes, it is ... what ...
COLIN: *(Going past her)* I got you something today ... Couldn't wait to give it to you ...
ANNETTE: *(Closing the door and following COLIN. She looks a bit annoyed)* Oh, yes?
COLIN: *(Taking a small package out of his pocket)* Mise Eire ...

(Pronounced "Misha Err-ah".)

ANNETTE: *(Puzzled)* What?
COLIN: That music, Damien was talking about ... Don't

you remember ... It's by Sean O' something-or-other ... He was ...

ANNETTE: *(Brushing past him)* Colin, I'm getting ready to go out ...

COLIN: *(It's obvious he's a bit "high")* Of course you remember ... That night up at Archway ... Damien was saying what a load of shit the band was ...

ANNETTE: *(Serious looking)* Colin ...

COLIN: *(Continues)* That we hadn't heard any real ... Real ... Irish music ... Don't you remember ... You should ... you were hanging on his every word ...

ANNETTE: Colin ...

COLIN: *(Won't be stopped)* I remember ... So I went out and got it ... *(Holds up the cassette)* And here it is ... "Mise Eire" ... The real McCoy ...

ANNETTE: *(Forced patience)* Colin, I really have to get ready ...

COLIN: Of course there's so much Damien thinks is a load of shit ... Have you ever noticed that it's one of his favourite words ... Only he doesn't say it like we do ...

ANNETTE: You're drunk.

COLIN: *(Flops down onto a sofa)* It depends upon what yard-stick you use to measure it by ... *(ANNETTE looks exasperated)* By my standards ... mine ... Yes, I am ... But by Damien's standards I'm barely tiddly ...

ANNETTE: Colin, please ...

COLIN: *(Continues)* Of course he has what's described as "license" ... hasn't he ... *(There is a pause in which we can see that ANNETTE just refuses to "play")* ... Well, hasn't he?

ANNETTE: *(Exiting to another room)* Oh, you're pissed ...

COLIN: *(Shouts)* License to kill, you might say ...

ANNETTE: *(Reappears instantly)* What did you say?

COLIN: I've brought you a present ... That's what I said ... *(Holds up the cassette)* Look ... a "pressy" ...

ANNETTE: *(Decides not to pursue the matter)* Oh, go home Colin ... you're drunk ...

(Returns to the other room.)

COLIN: Ha, home? ... I have no home ... I live in a hovel ... *(Stands up with effort and mumbles)* With pigs ... *(He goes and puts the tape on the machine and calls out)* Listen, Annette ... It really is beautiful ... I listened to it in the shop today ... listen ... *(Mise Eire starts to play) (After a time)* Isn't that beautiful ... *(He is talking half to himself)* He was right ... Damien ... But then he's nearly always, bloody right ... *(Shouts out to ANNETTE)* Isn't he?

ANNETTE: *(Returning)* I really do have to go, Colin ...

COLIN: *(Who is seated again)* I need to talk to you ..

ANNETTE: *(Exasperated, anything for a quiet life, she goes and sits facing COLIN)* Alright but I've only got five minutes, Ok?

COLIN: Yes, yes, fine ...

ANNETTE: *(After a pause)* Well? What?

COLIN: Annette ... what's happening ... to us?

ANNETTE: What do you mean, "happening"?

COLIN: You know what I mean ... Ever since ...

ANNETTE: Before you continue, Colin ... What was ever happening to us?

COLIN: *(Taken aback)* Oh, come on.

ANNETTE: Come on, nothing ... We had a lot in common ... we fell in together ...

COLIN: Fell in together? ... God, you make it sound so ... so ...

(Is lost for words.)

ANNETTE: So bloody "ordinary" ...
COLIN: But our "ideas" ... what we talked about ...

(He is totally lost.)

ANNETTE: And what did we talk about ... "Daddy's a bastard" ... "Oh, and so's Mummy" ... putting the world ...
COLIN: And that's it? ... That's all?
ANNETTE: That's all there was, Colin ...
COLIN: *(Shell-shocked)* But ... but ...

(Just stares helplessly at ANNETTE.)

ANNETTE: Oh, you mean we jumped in the sack together.
COLIN: *(Suddenly turns hard, vicious)* You, fucking ...
ANNETTE: *(Cuts him off sharply)* You say "whore", Colin and I swear I'll smash your skull in.
COLIN: *(Totally frustrated)* What am I supposed to say ...?
ANNETTE: *(Cool, deliberate)* Colin, you're not supposed to say anything ... You're not even supposed to be here ... *(Glances at her watch as she gets up from the seat)* I'm not supposed to be here ... *(As she goes to the door)* If you're driving I suggest you have some black coffee before you leave ... And pull the door after you ...

(Walks out.)

COLIN: *(Shouts)* It's him, isn't it?

ANNETTE: *(Coolly, doesn't look around)* ... Goodnight, Colin.

COLIN: It's Damien, isn't it ...

ANNETTE: Yes Colin ... It bloody is!

COLIN: Ha ... bloody is ... what a good description.

ANNETTE: Meaning what Colin?

COLIN: "Bloody is" is bloody ... ooops ... Freudian slip ... *(Instantly regrets)* I'm sorry, I'm sorry ... I didn't mean that ... I wouldn't ... I ... I ... *(Pleading)* Can't we talk ... can't we at least talk?

ANNETTE: Colin ...

COLIN: I can't just give up ... Oh I know he fascinates you.

ANNETTE: Colin ...

COLIN: No, Annette ... if we can't talk, at least let me ... What has happened to us, in just a few short weeks ... he's come into our lives ... correction ... he's come into my life, and I, as Damien might put it, "broke me bollox" to drag him into yours ... and didn't he just ... I knew that first night you know ... but then everybody in the fucking bar knew ... how could they not have ... he did everything short of taking his cock out ...

ANNETTE: You can stay here til you've sobered up.

COLIN: Annette ... *(ANNETTE exits, closing the door behind her. COLIN struggles up and rushes over to the tape machine and turns the tape up loud)* Mise – fucking – Eire ... Paddy – fucking – bastard ...

(COLIN lingers for a time. We can see that he is surveying the flat as though "for the last time". He exits from ANNETTE's flat.)
(The light fades.)

Scene Six

(A spot comes up downstage. A STREET. COLIN enters the spot. He is both drunk and exhausted/drained. He stops and closes his eyes tightly as though preventing himself from weeping.)

COLIN: Mise Eire ... I am Ireland ... *(He starts to address an imaginary DAMIEN)* That's what it means, isn't it, Damien ... Celtic and clean ... Down-trodden and dumped upon ... Isn't that right, Damien ... Poor little mother-fucking Ireland ... Land of Saints and Scholars ... Good craic, bishops and bombers ... where the songs are sad and the wars are merry ... and you've brought it all here, haven't you Damien ... and stupid sods like me are the key ... aren't we, Damien ... But then that's the beauty of it, isn't it ... who needs a huge army when there are whole regiments of pricks like me waiting to be tuned in and turned on ... Isn't that right ... You're fucking Annette and you're fucking me ... Fuck us all ... the long and the short and the tall ... A terrible beauty is born ... Well, we'll see ... *(Staggers out of spot)* We'll, fucking, see, you Paddy, frigging, bastard ...

(He exits. Spot goes down. Music fades as ...)

Scene Seven

(Light fades up on the bed in ANNETTE's room. DAMIEN and ANNETTE have just made love.)

ANNETTE: What's the matter, Damien?

DAMIEN: The matter? ... Not a lot ... *(He turns and looks at ANNETTE)* Well, everything's relevant, isn't it? Would you consider the fact that I'm a shit as "something the matter"?

ANNETTE: Is it Colin?

DAMIEN: No. It's nothing to do with that.

ANNETTE: Damien, were you out today?

DAMIEN: *(Non-plussed)* Out?

ANNETTE: Yes ... "out" ... You know what I mean.

DAMIEN: *(Laughs)* Oh, "out". As in "out plying my terrorist trade?"

ANNETTE: Stop being sarcastic ... You were the same last Tuesday.

DAMIEN: Last Tuesday?

ANNETTE: Yea ... After that business in Enfield.

DAMIEN: You mean after me and big Louis cased that barracks.

ANNETTE: *(Grabbing the opportunity to be, and remain, light)* Do you know something ... I wouldn't be surprised if you really had a member called Big Louis ...

DAMIEN: Wouldn't you?

ANNETTE: No ... And you mentioning him is a clever subterfuge.

DAMIEN: Do you really think that I'm that clever?

ANNETTE: Cleverer.

DAMIEN: How's this for clever ... I'm really a temporarily employed dispatch clerk in a arse-hole of a warehouse just this side of Fulham and I've been giving you a load of bullshit to get inside your knickers.

ANNETTE: *(Pretends to "consider" this)* Ummm ... Well, personally I think that that is just a teeny-wheeny bit too James Bondish to be credible.

DAMIEN: Do you, indeed?

ANNETTE: Yea ... If you were really a dispatch clerk working just this side of Fulham you would have told me that you were, *(Considers for a moment)* Now, let me see ...

DAMIEN: An IRA man on active service?

ANNETTE: Why ... is that what you tell all the girls?

DAMIEN: No ... I usually let them tell me.

ANNETTE: Do you enjoy teasing me?

DAMIEN: *(Suddenly serious)* ... Annette ...

(Stops)

ANNETTE: *(Notices and reacts to the changed mood)* Yea?

DAMIEN: Does it matter to you ... What I am?

ANNETTE: *(Throws her arms around him)* Oh no, darling no ... *(She kisses him passionately and then pulls back, smiling)* Actually that's not "quite" true ... I "admire" you for what you are.

DAMIEN: *(Deadpan)* "Admire" me?

ANNETTE: *(Quite animated, excited almost)* Yes ... your commitment, your "passion" ... God, when I think back on all the meetings I've attended over the last two years ... We were saving seals when the people of Belfast and Derry were being mowed down in their own streets ... On the day Bobby Sands was buried I was spraying red dye over a woman's coat in Oxford Street ... Whoopy shit!

DAMIEN: *(Subdued awkward)* Annette.

ANNETTE: Not another word ... Coffee ... I'll get coffee ... And it's not decaffeinated ... To hell with the risks ...

(She exits to make the coffee. DAMIEN is despondent, his head in his hands.)

DAMIEN: Shit, shit, shit, shit.

ANNETTE: *(Offstage)* Did you say something, darling?

DAMIEN: *(Shouts into her)* ... Just talking to myself. *(In normal voice)* Just doing a spot of self-analysis.

ANNETTE: It's the first sign of madness, they say.

DAMIEN: Or idiocy.

ANNETTE: What?

DAMIEN: *(Almost bad-temperedly)* Nothing ...

(He sits pounding a fist into his other hand. He looks/is fretful. ANNETTE enters with the coffee. DAMIEN is sitting staring at the ground.)

ANNETTE: Here we ...

DAMIEN: *(Very suddenly which takes ANNETTE aback)* I love you, Annette.

ANNETTE: *(Kneels on floor in front of him and speaks very tenderly)* Well ... *(Pauses, composes herself)* Funny you should say that because I ...

DAMIEN: *(Looks up for the first time. He looks nervous)* If I was to say that I'm thinking of going back to Ireland, what would you say? ...

ANNETTE: *(Gently)* I'd say I've never been to Ireland.

DAMIEN: *(Almost in a whisper)* Good. And if I said there are things you assume about me that aren't true. What would you say?

ANNETTE: What do you mean? Like what?

DAMIEN: *(Clearly, almost too loudly)* I'm a fraud.

ANNETTE: *(Unsure)* What?

DAMIEN: I'm a fraud ... On the day Bobby Sands was buried I had three horses up in a Yankee and was over the frigging moon.

ANNETTE: A Yankee?

DAMIEN: It's a sort of bet with four horses ...

ANNETTE: *(Almost screams)* To hell with the bloody Yankee ... What are you telling me?

DAMIEN: I let you believe what you wanted to believe.

ANNETTE: Damien, what are you trying to say?

DAMIEN: What Colin told you, he was wrong.

ANNETTE: About what? I don't understand.

DAMIEN: I'm a dispatch clerk ... pure and simple.

ANNETTE: Damien, you don't have to do this to me. You can trust me.

DAMIEN: I'm a dispatch clerk. Please Annette I've been trying to tell you for weeks. Annette, I love you.

ANNETTE: Everything you just said It's true, isn't it?

DAMIEN: I love you.

ANNETTE: *(Screams)* Stop saying that ... Especially about ...

(She pulls her dressing gown more tightly around herself.)

DAMIEN: *(Goes a step towards her)* Annette, please.

When did I ever say I was?

ANNETTE: And to think that I actually thought I loved you ... You're disgusting.

DAMIEN: Did you?

ANNETTE: Just shows you what a fool I've been.

DAMIEN: So what's hurt ... Your heart or your pride?

ANNETTE: My heart ... My heart? ... Is that what you were looking for in my knickers ... was it? Or was it all just a good laugh?

DAMIEN: And what were you looking for in me, eh?

ANNETTE: You? ... There is no "you" ... Isn't that what you're telling me ... That you're a fiction?

DAMIEN: And isn't that what you wanted?

ANNETTE: It was the reality I wanted.

DAMIEN: And what about the dispatch clerk ... His reality ... That's the nature of reality ... It tends to come in "clerk-sized" packages ... But then spoilt little middle-class girls don't have clerk-sized appetites, do they?

(At this point her portable phone starts to ring.)

ANNETTE: *(Strides over and slaps DAMIEN across the face)* How dare you ...

DAMIEN: *(Pulling her raised hand down)* You'd better get that ... It's likely Mummy ...

(ANNETTE answers the phone, all the time glaring at DAMIEN. She listens for a moment before addressing DAMIEN.)

ANNETTE: It's for you ...

(She tosses the phone towards him.)

DAMIEN: *(Takes the phone and listens for a short time before speaking into it)* Fuck off, Colin ... *(He turns the phone off, tries to calm things down)* Annette ... I do love you ... Me.

ANNETTE: *(Scornfully)* The clerk.

DAMIEN: Will you shut up about the fucking clerk.

ANNETTE: It was your metaphor.

DAMIEN: And what was Damien the IRA man ... Your wet dream?

ANNETTE: *(Slowly)* You filthy bastard ... Get out ... I need a bath.

DAMIEN: Annette, I love you, for Christsake.

ANNETTE: "For Christsake" ... What was that ... A cheap Americanism or did it come from your deep Celtic soul ... I take it that that is what you have ... *(She moves towards the door and opens it)* Now, get out! *(DAMIEN goes to speak but cannot find anything to say. He leaves, dejected, stopping by ANNETTE at the door for a moment. She doesn't look at him. The words still won't come. He exits. ANNETTE slams the door on his back. As soon as he's left, she buries her face in her hands)* Damien, oh Damien.

(Lights fade.)

Scene Eight

(The bedroom of the lodging house. The lights come up, slowly. It is much later the same night. BRIAN is lying on his bed fiddling with his knife. After a time we hear

people on the landing outside. They are mumbling, bumping into walls, and obviously drunk.)

MICHAEL: *(Offstage)* You go on in there ... You'll be alright ... Go on ... Go on ...
COLIN: *(Mumbling off)* I'm alright.
MICHAEL: *(Off)* Fingers down your throat, you'll feel better. *(We hear a door being closed. BRIAN lies still, watching the door. It opens and MICHAEL enters. He is unsteady on his feet)* Jasus, what a night ... What a frigging night ... The poor wee bastard's in bits ...
BRIAN: *(Coolly)* Oh Yeah?
MICHAEL: Aye ... That bastard, Damien ... And bastard's the only word for him ... He's only gone and nicked his fucking girlfriend ...
BRIAN: Wot ... Annette?
MICHAEL: Aye, whatever her name is ...
BRIAN: Well, don't say I didn't tell you ...
MICHAEL: What? ... About Annette?
BRIAN: Your mate ...
MICHAEL: Who? ... Damien? He's no fucking, mate of mine.
BRIAN: Well ... 'ee's Irish, i'nnet 'ee ...
MICHAEL: What's that go to do with it? ... I'm Irish, for Christsake ...
BRIAN: Yeah ... exactly ...
MICHAEL: *(Somewhat perturbed)* And what the fuck does that mean ... "Yeah, exactly"?
BRIAN: *(Who, until now, has been lying casually on his back, suddenly gets up onto his elbow)* ... The bastard's a fucking terrorist ... I've told you.

MICHAEL: *(A bit hesitant)* Now, come on, Brian ...

BRIAN: What about all these weird messages the bastard gets, eh? And the packages? ... Do you know what they say ... "There's none so blind as he". Isn't that right, Michael?

MICHAEL: *(Emphatically indicating himself.)* What are you saying? ...

BRIAN: *(Lying back again)* I'm not saying fuck all ... But do you remember that morning they done the recruiting office?

MICHAEL: *(Quickly, almost anxious)* Yeah.

BRIAN: You was talking about hanging the bastards, then.

MICHAEL: Yeah ... So?

BRIAN: But if you didn't know who they was ... Or didn't want to ... Well ... there is no question of 'anging then ... *(Turns and looks directly at MICHAEL)* Is there?

MICHAEL: *(Emphasizing the point)* ... Listen ... I don't give a fuck who it is ... And I've no time for that bollox Damien, anyroad ... but don't get me wrong ... If you're right I'd hang the bastard.

BRIAN: *(Dismissively)* Bollox.

MICHAEL: What do you mean, "bollox"?

BRIAN: *(Looking at MICHAEL)* It's the ol' "shit to a blanket" story, innit? ... 'ee's Irish, and you're Irish.

MICHAEL: *(Indignant)* Fuck off ... No way ... I'm ... There's Colin ... *(He gets up and opens the door and COLIN staggers in)* ... Are you Ok, kid?

COLIN: *(Looks deadly pale, he heads towards his bed)* Yeah, yeah ...

MICHAEL: *(Addresses BRIAN)* Poor wee bastard ... You want to have seen the show he made of me the night ...

Fucking crying he was ... *(By now COLIN has gone and flopped, face-forward onto his bed)* ... And bloody Molloy there ...

BRIAN: Yeah?

MICHAEL: Aye ... The first time in the bloody bar and he comes marching in, fucking crying, and lands up beside me ... Molloy thought he was a fruit, or something.

BRIAN: *(Addresses COLIN)* OK, mate? ... Where's your pal then? *(COLIN mumbles)* Damien, ... Your buddy ...

COLIN: *(Rises on his elbows)* He ... he ... *(Tears welling)* Bastard ...

(Flops down again.)

MICHAEL: *(Addressing BRIAN)* Ach, leave the poor wee fellow alone ... He's broken hearted ...

BRIAN: *(Suddenly throws his knife at the door. It sticks in it, and he gets up to retrieve it)* Fucking shut it ...

MICHAEL: *(Taken aback)* Waat?

BRIAN: *(Turning on MICHAEL)* Where do you fucking stand?

MICHAEL: What do you mean?

BRIAN: *(Threatening)* Wot I, fucking say ... Do you support those bastards, or don't you?

MICHAEL: *(Shaken)* No ...

BRIAN: Good.

MICHAEL: *(Nervous of the direction he sees things are going in)* But, Brian ...

BRIAN: *(Comes and stands over him. He is still playing with the knife)* 'ere we go ... 'ere we bleeding go ...

MICHAEL: What do you mean?

BRIAN: Know something, Michael ... For a bloke who's usually pretty quick you've slowed right down to a walking pace tonight ... One might even say a crawling bleeding pace.

MICHAEL: *(Stands up abruptly. This leaves both men face to face)* Are you saying that I'm a crawler?

BRIAN: I'm saying that every time we touch on that bastard, Damien, you go all vague like ...

(Just at that COLIN pipes up. This takes both MICHAEL and BRIAN by surprise.)

COLIN: *(Half mumbles)* Bastard.

BRIAN: *(Looks around at him and goes and sits on the edge of his bed)* Who's that, then, Colin ... Damien?

COLIN: *(Close always to tears)* I phoned up ...

BRIAN: But I thought 'ee was your mate ...

COLIN: *(Carries on his own narrative)* That time I left here ... I phoned Annette ... *(Looks up directly at BRIAN)* Do you know what she said?

BRIAN: *(Puts on "kindly" voice)* What? ... You tell me, ol' son.

COLIN: That I couldn't come around because her mother was up ... It's always, "her mother's up" ...

BRIAN: *(Caressing his head)* Oh yeah?

COLIN: But I caught her out ... I'm not stupid, you know ...

BRIAN: Nobody says you was ...

COLIN: I phoned her mother ... Her mother ... In bloody Cheltenham. *(Starts to put on a false laugh)* Do you know what she asked me?

BRIAN: Wot?

COLIN: Could I ask Annette ... *(Pause)* Could I ask bitch ... to phone her ... Phone her ... in Cheltenham ... Me ... ask her ... *(Laughs again.)* She hasn't seen her in months ... bloody months.

BRIAN: Bitch.

COLIN: *(Still forced laughing/crying)* And do you know something else?

MICHAEL: *(Who has watched all this with great discomfort)* Just leave the lad a ...

BRIAN: *(Snaps)* Shut it ... *(Returns his "kindly" attention to COLIN)* Go on, kid ...

COLIN: *(As though not having noticed the exchange)* I rang up ... *(Pause)* ... I rang up ... Annette ...

(Stops)

BRIAN: And?

COLIN: *(Very quietly, defeated)* She put him on the line ...

BRIAN: *(Equally quietly)* Who? ... Damien?

MICHAEL: *(Can't take it any more)* For Jasus sake don't you know rightly who the lad means ... leave the wee fella alone. All you're doing is tormenting him ...

BRIAN: I was wondering when you were going to jump to his defense.

MICHAEL: I'm jumping to nobody's defense.

BRIAN: Well nobody's in this room, you're not ...

MICHAEL: I wish to fuck you'd stop talking in riddles, Brian ... All I'm saying is that I've heard all this down in the pub and I don't see the point in putting him through it over and over again.

BRIAN: Oh, don't you?

MICHAEL: There you go again ... I'm telling you, I wish to Christ I'd never laid eyes on that Damien ... Better still ... I wish to Christ he had turned out to be a frigging Pakistani that night ... There's been nothing but a bad atmosphere since he landed in here.

BRIAN: I'm sure you do ... then you wouldn't have to go through the strain of turning the blind eye.

MICHAEL: Listen ... I've less time for them bastards than you do ... Do you have any idea what it's like for Irish people in this country after some of them carry out a bombing ... Do you?

BRIAN: Who gives a fuck ... We're too busy collecting our own people into body-bags to have much time to worry about the finer feelings of fucking Paddys.

MICHAEL: So ... we're all guilty?

BRIAN: You know what they say ... "They also serve who stand by and turn a blind eye" ...

MICHAEL: And that's what you say I'm doing? ... If I thought for a minute that Damien ...

BRIAN: If you thought for a minute ... Knock it off, mate ... Do you think he's on the up and up ... And what do you think about all this with Colin's bird ... *(At this point we notice that COLIN, until now very still, almost dazed, sparks up into attention, MICHAEL and BRIAN don't notice)* Do you think it's just her body he's interested in? Have you ever noticed the sort of women any of these terrorist groups use ... They're always middle-class, well connected ... You never hear of them getting caught up with bleeding tarts out of Tescos, do you?

MICHAEL: Ach, come on now, Brian ... So he's nicked

Colin's girlfriend ... Ok, he deserves a smack on the mouth for being so devious ...

COLIN: *(Quietly, calmly)* It's true ...

(Up until this point MICHAEL and BRIAN have almost forgotten COLIN's presence. There is a silence as they both look at COLIN and then exchange glances.)

BRIAN: Wot?

COLIN: Damien ... The bastard is in the IRA.

MICHAEL: Are you sure, son?

BRIAN: *(Snaps)* Don't you fucking start again.

COLIN: He told me to fuck off ...

BRIAN: What?

COLIN: When I phoned Annette ... He told me to fuck off.

BRIAN: About this IRA stuff ...

COLIN: *(Not listening, crying)* I liked him ... I liked him ...

BRIAN: *(Looks over at MICHAEL)* Yeah ... Well so does Annette ...

MICHAEL: Will you ...

BRIAN: *(Over MICHAEL)* So does Michael, here ..

MICHAEL: That's not what I said ...

BRIAN: Oh yeah? ... Wot the fuck, are you saying, Michael? ...

MICHAEL: *(Excited, panicked)* I've told you ...

BRIAN: *(Quickly)* Oh yeah, you've told me a lot of bleeding things ... Like you'd hang the bastards ...

MICHAEL: *(Quickly, desperately)* Yeah ...

BRIAN: *(Cuts in)* So we'll 'ave no problems with you

when the bastard comes in, then?

MICHAEL: *(Somewhat relieved)* Problems? ... It's him who has the fucking problems, mate ...

COLIN: *(Suddenly goes to get out of bed)* I've got to talk to Annette ... I've got to tell her ...

BRIAN: *(Restrains him)* About what?

COLIN: He's using her ... Just like me ...

BRIAN: You lie quiet, mate ... Ok? ... We'll 'andle 'im ... *(Turns to MICHAEL)* ... Won't we ... Mick?

MICHAEL: *(To COLIN)* Yes, son ... You just lie quiet ... He won't get away with it ... He's been looking for a bloody nose since the day and hour he moved in here ... *(He addresses BRIAN)* Did I tell you about the morning I was trying to be friendly to him ... The little pup ... and him just in the Country five minutes ... he ...

(We hear someone approaching. BRIAN lifts his hand to stop MICHAEL talking.)

BRIAN: Ok, Michael ... Stow it.

(DAMIEN enters. He looks at COLIN on the bed and then at MICHAEL and BRIAN. He starts to take his coat off.)

DAMIEN: Well, lads ...
BRIAN: Good time, then?
DAMIEN: *(Patiently exasperated)* Well, lads ... ?

(He has no sooner uttered these words than BRIAN grabs him by the throat. BRIAN is wielding the knife. DAMIEN knees BRIAN in the balls and BRIAN drops to the ground.)

(As soon as this happens, MICHAEL jumps up and hits DAMIEN smack in the face. The blow drives DAMIEN back and he falls across the bed. BRIAN has recovered by now and jumps up and pounces upon DAMIEN, who is still on the bed.)

BRIAN: IRA fucking bastard ...

(He starts pummeling DAMIEN.)

DAMIEN: *(In the midst of being attacked)* Hang ... Hold on ... Please ...

(MICHAEL joins the attack.)

MICHAEL: *(Whilst hitting DAMIEN)* Fucking whore ... Bastard ...

(The noise and sudden activity revives COLIN.)

DAMIEN: *(Trying to protect himself with his arms)* Please ... no ... no ... I'm not ... I'm not ...
BRIAN: *(Still hitting him)* Not, fucking wot?
MICHAEL: *(Holding onto BRIAN's shoulder for balance and still hitting out)* We'll teach you, you bastard ... Won't we, Brian ... We'll teach him.
DAMIEN: I swear to Jesus ... Please ... On my mother's life ...

(They continue a relentless assault.)

BRIAN: Wouldn't have the balls, would you?

(DAMIEN continues to plead, helplessly. During this, COLIN has sat up and taken the scene in. He looks half dazed. He gets up and approaches in an almost somnambulant fashion. The closer he gets the more excited, animated he becomes. He eventually joins in, laughing.)

COLIN: *(Attempting to hit DAMIEN)* You bastard ... You lying, fucking, pigging bastard ...

(In the struggle, DAMIEN rolls off the bed. The three of them start to kick him as he lies on the floor.)

BRIAN: *(Each word emphasized by a kick)* Still like fucking niggers though, don't you ...

(DAMIEN is weakening ...)

MICHAEL: Fucking traitor ...

(At this stage, from the audience's point of view, DAMIEN is out of sight behind the bed.)
(Light [from an overturned lamp?] is shining up into the faces of his attackers. They are quite manic.)

BRIAN: *(Words per blow)* Nigger ... loving ... fucking ... bastard ...

(At this point the door is flung open and MRS. SOMERS enters.)

MRS. SOMERS: *(Rushing towards the scene)* Here, here, here, ... What's going on here? ... *(The attack ceases. MRS. SOMERS bends down towards DAMIEN)* Damien .. Damien, lad ... *(She pauses, examines him)* Oh my God ... Oh my God ...

(There is a silence.)
(COLIN starts to giggle.)

MICHAEL: *(Walks out mumbling)* "Shit, shit, shit."

BRIAN: *(Who remains standing and staring into MRS. SOMERS' face)* Nigger lover ...

MRS. SOMERS: *(Who is gob-smacked and staring at BRIAN)* Why?

BRIAN: *(Still maniacal, as lights fade)* Nigger lover.

FINAL CURTAIN

PROP PRESET LIST

4 Beds with top & bottom sheet, 1 yellow blanket, 1 plaid blanket (check all spike marks)
- #1 (C) 2 pillows, stool left of head with 3 books (3rd world economics on top), sweater & jacket, center shoes under bed, on foot of bed: open spiral pad (written page) black pencil, open labor party book.
- #2 (B) 2 pillows, locker at head with unbuttoned shirt & united tie, chair facing stage left at foot - set a bit away from bed (brown dress shoes under chair) with sports jacket over back.
- #3 (M) 2 pillows, slippers underneath, trunk at head.
- #4 (D) 2 pillows, suitcase, 2 packages at stage right end (foot), 3 towels folded on top of suitcase, bed cover reaches floor.

Square table (check spikes)
 Football pools, pen (near stage right chair).
 2 chairs (1 stage right, 1 stage left of table which is pushed in ½ way).

Kitchen unit (preset onstage)
 R section top: teacups, saucers, mugs, beige Damien mug.
 C section bottom: tray, plate with 4 triangles of sliced bananas, margarine sandwiches with tea towel over them.
 L section top: key, teapots, picture of Jack in frame.
 L section bottom: radio.
 On left wall: telephone.
 Prop handoff: electric kettle, frying pan & scraper, damp rag, Mrs. Somers coat, scarf, hat, pocketbook.

PADDYWACK 113

Round table with 3 chairs: R/L/S (check spikes)
    On table: creamer with milk, granulated sugar in bowl with spoon, open newspaper, teacup, saucer, spoon (with small amount of regular tea with milk, set stage right of paper - set near stage left chair), teapot with cozy.

Pub Unit (offstage)
    Sherry glass (full shot), 2 whiskey glasses (shot full).

Annette's unit (offstage) I.4
    Sofa with Annette's jacket (stage left back), pillows.
    Behind sofa: cassette player on table (remove cassette, check volume down - on radio mode), garbage pail (R), lamp & set dressing - books.
    Coffee table with Economist (open), glass of wine, Annette's keys.
    Side table (L): portable phone.

Annette's unit I.7
    Strike pillows, set of 2 whiskey glasses on stage right end of coffee table.

Stage right prop table
    (I.3) Plate, fork, spoon, knife, mug (Michael)
    (I.3) Plate with 3 slices of banana & ½ piece of whole wheat toast, fork, spoon, knife, mug (Brian)
    (I.4) Rejection letter, nuclear dumping article, bottle wine (no cork) (Mice)
    (1.4) 1 empty wine glass, 1 wine glass with 1 sip of wine (Annette)
    (I.6) 1 empty beer glass, 1 beer glass with 1 sip, ashtray (Annette)
    (I.6) Set cigs & lighter in Colin's jacket

(I.7) 2 whiskey glasses (small amount of liquid in one) (Mice for coffee table)
(I.7) Whiskey bottle (liquid reaches back label), 1 whiskey glass (Mice for round table - set near stage right chair)
(II.1) Payphone coins (Colin)
(II.1) Coffee mug (Damien)
(II.3) Cup & saucer (attached), newspaper (handoff to Mrs. Somers)
(II.5) Purse, wallet (empty), pounds, lipstick, compact, blushcase, Kleenex, belt, cigs, lighter (Annette)
(II.6) Underwear, pants with belt, shirt, socks, shoes, jacket (Damien)
(II.6) 2 coffee mugs with coffee (Annette)

Down right vom prop table
(I.5) Newspaper with bomb headline (Brian)
(II.2) Parcel (Mrs. Somers)
(II.2) Evening standard newspaper - remove clipped page (Brian)
(II.4) Economics of Chaos book, spiral pad, red pencil, thesis paper (Colin)

Stage left prop table
(I.5) Playing cards, unopened beer can (Damien)
(I.6) Cigarettes, lighter (Damien)
(I.6) Sherry glass (full shot), 2 whiskey glasses
(II.2) Magazine (Michael)
(II.5) Cassette in case with label (Colin)

Personal prop
(II.2) Eyeglasses (Mrs. Somers)
(II.4) Switchblade (Brian)

PADDYWACK

INTERMISSION CHANGE / ACT II PRESETS

Strike work shoes from under chair #2 (Brian) - Costumes
Clean out jacket, shirt from #2 trunk (Brian) - Costumes
Strike Michael's shoes under bed #3 - Costumes
Set portable phone on stage left prop table
Strike whiskey, 2 glasses off round table
Strike Colin's Economics of Chaos book, pad, off stool next to bed #1, set onto down right vom prop table with red pencil.
Annette's unit up, wall onstage, kitchen unit on
Clean spike marks on chairs around the round table (R is one for Mrs. Somers - move it up stage, check both upstage chairs are between table legs)
Charge glo tape on down left corner for Brian in II.7

SET ANNETTE'S UNIT (II.5)
Sweater on center of sofa, cassette player behind sofa / Annette's shoes: 1 under center, 1 in front of sofa (stage left end) / Reset pillows on unit / Keys set on coffee table / Portable phone on lamp table / Empty garbage pail

ANNETTE'S UNIT (II.6)
Bring bed out / Set wedges, 4 pillows / Stage left side - Annette's robe (set by Annette) / Stage right side - Damien's underwear, pants, shoes, socks, shirt, jacket (set by Damien)

PERISHABLES: Banana, whole wheat bread, thin white bread, milk, sugar (granulated), tea/coffee, sherry (grape juice), wine (grape juice), Heineken, whiskey (ice tea), Irish breakfast tea, bottled water, fake beer.